Managing Conflict
From the Inside Out

Managing Conflict

From the Inside Out

Marc Robert

Learning Concepts

Distributed by
UNIVERSITY ASSOCIATES

*Managing Conflict
from the Inside Out*

Library of Congress Catalog Card Number: 81-70980
ISBN 0-89384-065-3
Printed in the United States of America

Learning Concepts
Austin, Texas

Distributed by University Associates, Inc.
8517 Production Avenue
P.O. Box 26240
San Diego, California 92126

Preface

I have written this book for the primary purpose of encouraging the reader to become more aware of his or her power and responsibility in managing interpersonal conflict. A secondary purpose was to offer a broad assortment of specific, field-tested ideas that would be readily adaptable to the reader's personal and professional world. It is my hope that this approach will contribute in a practical way to the eradication of the unnecessary pain of mishandled conflict situations.

My fond appreciation goes to my colleagues and friends who contributed ideas and encouragement by personal example as well as by direct suggestion. Special thanks go to my editor, Mary Kitzmiller, for the helpful and nonconflictive way in which she offered technical assistance, and to Florence Mendeloff, who interrupted her retirement to give the manuscript an intelligent and meticulous typing.

Los Angeles   Marc Robert
December 1981

Table of Contents

Introduction

As implied by its title, this book is based on the premise that interpersonal conflict is best handled by those who have a clear sense of themselves and of their uniqueness. This admitted bias has been reinforced countless times in training workshops, seminars, and counseling sessions in which I have watched participants swallowing whole the popular self-help packages without spending nearly enough time investigating whether or not the prescriptions were compatible with their unique values, needs, and styles. As a result, their newly acquired but noninternalized skills disappeared almost immediately in their first brushes with real-life situations.

Because of the disruptive—sometimes frightening—nature of interpersonal conflict, skill in conflict management requires enough realistic self-study to make appropriate behavioral choices, even under intense pressure. This inside-out approach is based on the following beliefs:

- To the extent that we lack awareness of how others perceive us and of how we are likely to react to conflict stressors, we are handicapped in our ability to manage conflict effectively.
- Basic strategies for managing various kinds of conflict can be learned, but they will work effectively only when they fit the style of the person using them.
- Though some conflict is positive and produces growth, much of it is unnecessary and unwarranted and can be productively avoided.
- Sometimes it is not possible to manage conflict in a way that makes everyone a winner. Some conflicts—although not amenable to negotiation or problem solving—still must be dealt with. Specific training is available to assist in handling such situations, but mastering the skill is not easy without considerable practice.

1

- Because a person may occasionally feel like a "loser" in certain conflict situations, some strategies for dealing with such feelings should be developed.

Managing Conflict from the Inside Out is organized to deal with these basic premises in ways that will encourage positive introspection, selectivity, and success. The continuous focus is the development of a personal system for managing conflict through awareness, choice, and appropriate success-oriented action.

To receive maximum value from this book, the reader is encouraged to follow the sequence of conflict awareness and self-study described in Chapters 1 and 2 *before* examining the strategies and tactics suggested in subsequent chapters. This procedure is recommended to avoid the perennial self-help trap of developing answers before adequately understanding the questions.

Chapter 1

Conflict Consciousness

You can run but you can't hide.
Joe Louis

The rapid changes of the twentieth century have increased human conflict to the point that our sensibilities toward each other are becoming numb. The human capacity for adaptation may be working against our social relationships as we passively accept conditions that are not conducive to the effective resolution of interpersonal differences. Just as we adapt to bad air, tasteless food, polluted water, congested cities, and loud noise, we are also becoming callous and indifferent to the factors in our environment that are setting us at one another's throats. If future shock had really shocked us, we would have been far better off. Instead, the future sneaked up so insidiously that we were lulled into accepting the unacceptable and now must exert conscious and determined efforts to recapture our awareness of what it takes to get along.

The first step in developing an effective personal system of conflict management requires resensitizing ourselves to what *has happened* and what *is happening* around us. Take a moment to sharpen your sense of the change and conflict that may be disrupting your personal world.

ENVIRONMENTAL PROBLEMS

The following twelve items describe some of the problems in our environment that contribute to conflict in Western society today. Consider them in the light of how they affect you and the significant others in your life.

1. More Issues than Answers

Events of the past few years are producing an increasing number of value-laden controversies that tend to polarize responsible

3

people. Powerful emotions come into play as points of view collide over issues such as abortion, affirmative-action programs, the feminist movement, personal rights, discrimination and reverse discrimination, capital punishment and law and order, smokers and clean air, test-tube babies, pornography and sexual freedom, school integration and mandatory busing, taxation, labor-management problems, and life support and the right to die. The list is growing every day.

These issues produce turmoil within families, schools, churches, and job environments in overt and subtle ways. As conflict surfaces, sides are chosen and relationships are strained or even destroyed.

2. Money Tripping and Materialism

Despite a general rise in the standard of living, many people feel overtaxed and underpaid as they watch with anxiety the erosion of their purchasing power. Yet they are unable to resist the power of advertisements, which daily seduce them into deeper debt. The relentless acquisition of material goods and the energy required to service and maintain them contribute significantly to the general malaise of the times. Automobile ownership alone can be an open-ended source of conflict. Think about accidents, insurance, service warranties, inadequate repairs, used-car dealers, licenses, teen-age drivers, traffic tickets, inadequate fuel, traffic jams, etc. Then add a few more problems: charge accounts (not to mention lost or stolen credit cards), attempts to balance the checkbook, family conflicts about how to spend money, appliances that break down, accumulation of more possessions than the time needed to care for them, and concern about personal appearance. Are we confusing standard of living with quality of life?

3. Family Discord and Distress

Traditionally, the family has been the one institution we could count on. It was a refuge—the glue that held our social fiber together. However, for a variety of reasons, the glue has lost some of its strength. Divorce, serial marriages, nonconnubial life styles, gay rights, increased mobility, contraception, abortion, and other factors are producing conflict where there used to be harmony and accord. No longer are disorganization and delinquency limited to minorities and the poor. Family disorganization is spreading throughout middle-class society in towns, suburbs, and rural communities. The middle-class family—in terms of working mothers, number of adults in the home, single-parent families, or children born out of wedlock—resembles the low-income family of two decades ago (Bronfenbrenner, 1976).

4. Law and the Courts

Courts are jammed and lawyers are proliferating. Almost anything is fair game for litigation, yet the legal system seems unable to function effectively. There seems to be no relief in sight as legal disputes increase in response to affirmative action, civil rights, divorce, increased crime, school busing, collective bargaining, libel and slander, automobile accidents, medical malpractice, and countless other demands of lawsuit-conscious citizens.

5. Chemical Escapism

The amount of ingested chemicals (both legal and illegal) is increasing. Mind-altering substances, including alcohol, tranquilizers, marijuana, and other drugs, are affecting the behavior of growing numbers of people. Instead of reducing conflict, our search for artificial tranquility through chemistry seems to aggravate the problems between the users and their social environment. Even graffiti reflects cultural trends. Recently a wall was decorated with the slogan, "Reality is an escape for those who can't handle drugs."

6. Doing Our Own Thing

The past twenty years have seen an inexorable cultural shift from recognizable social movements toward a greater focus on self. In the "good old days"—before TV, human-rights movements, and increasing affluence—most people were either blatantly mistreated or were so busy scrambling to make a living that they had neither the time nor inclination to even think about "doing their own thing." According to many scholars and observers of the social scene (Glasser, 1972; Schur, 1977), we are now living in the "me" society. As more people acquire enough leisure and affluence to explore their personal-growth needs, their own needs, rights, and values start to clash with those of others. As personal growth becomes self-absorption and as awareness turns into selfishness, conflicts are certain to increase.

7. Unthinkable Thoughts

Shoved back into the recesses of our consciousness is the thought that, sometime, someone may push the nuclear button. Concern about this terminal conflict is kept alive by the media. Add to this the prospect of global famine, massive energy shortages, international monetary collapse, allegations of mind control by governments, catastrophic illness, air pollution, political terrorism, and other mind-boggling problems. These thoughts (which, fortunately, the conscious mind blocks out most of the time) are probably raising our blood pressure and may be contributing to the general waspishness and escapism of the times.

8. Anti-Institutional Bias

Cynicism and lack of confidence seem to be the prevailing attitudes toward government and other large institutions. Many people behave as though they are at war with their government and try to use the initiative process and the polls to eliminate taxes and "throw the rascals out."

Within large public and private organizations a continuing struggle is in process as individual members and employees seek to meet their personal needs, which are often in conflict with the demands of the institutions that employ them.

The general mistrust of *bigness* in both public and private sectors is reflected by increasingly belligerent public sentiment.

9. Increasing Crime and Violence

According to available data, your chances of becoming a victim of violence or of white-collar or blue-collar crime have increased sharply. Violence on television and a succession of wars electronically delivered to our living rooms have brutalized and desensitized many people. Violence in sports is on the increase and is often tacitly condoned.

10. Overcrowding

As more people enter the middle class, they compete for housing, material goods, recreation, desirable jobs, and work locations. Their desire to be in the "best" places causes waiting lines at theaters, restaurants, and sporting events; parking problems; traffic jams; and oversubscribed recreation areas. Only the wealthy now have the means to get away from the "madding crowd." The poor and middle class fight the crowds or do without. This is not a judgment, but a concern that conflicts will proliferate as more people attempt to occupy limited space.

11. Personal and Social Isolation

Personal isolation has increased in spite of overcrowding and overpopulation. Consider the proliferation of stereo headsets on joggers as they shut out the world. The automobile is a steel cocoon housing its isolated occupant. Freeways are built over and around large sections of cities. Drive-in banks, theaters, restaurants, and churches reduce person-to-person contact. We often find ourselves communicating with computers instead of people. Conversation is becoming a lost art as people vegetate in front of the TV tube. We are not getting enough practice in social interaction; and when interpersonal conflicts occur, it is no wonder that they are handled badly.

12. Communication Overload and Abuse

Each of the items mentioned so far is magnified and aggravated by the relentless bombardment of the communication media. As TV and radio bring every issue into our homes and automobiles, we become better informed. We also become more aware of threats to our security and well-being.

The mixed blessing of instantaneous communication increases our susceptibility to conflict as we hear the human voice used more to hurt, hinder, and exasperate than to soothe, satisfy, or inform. Perhaps rudeness is not the *rule* in the affairs of this world, but if our sensibilities become jaded, our abilities to handle conflict in humane and positive ways will continue to erode.

This brief list of environmental producers of conflict suggests that in order to avoid becoming a casualty, one must recognize, understand, and—to some degree—accept the contentious energy of our times. Awareness helps replace our unrealistic anxieties with legitimate and manageable fears. The alternative to awareness is too often the subtle onset of stress-related pain and illness.

When I discover people who seem uniquely successful in managing the conflict in their lives, I watch what they do and listen to what they say about their personal view of reality. A composite of their statements and ideas about conflict sounds something like this:

There is a lot going on in my life that I can't control or get away from. When I get up in the morning I know that I will probably run into a conflict that I don't want or need.

I'm probably not the target of most events that aggravate me.

Life is unpredictable and unfair, and this world is far from ideal.

I usually make my own messes.

These are the good old days—there's no going back. I try to stay in the here and now because it's all I have.

However, the composite also includes the following types of positive statements:

I have options about what to do when things around me aren't going well.

The more I become aware of possible conflicts, the better choices I make.

There are many ways to increase personal awareness of the conflict in one's life. The Conflict-Consciousness Survey will help you communicate with yourself about the possible sources of conflict in your life that are costing you unnecessary amounts of time and energy. Find a quiet place to work and avoid discussing your responses with anyone until you have finished.

CONFLICT-CONSCIOUSNESS SURVEY

Part 1

General Conflict Awareness Questions

Read each of the following questions and talk to yourself about them. Write any thoughts that you may have in the space provided. If a question is not meaningful to you, skip it and go on to the next one.

1. Recall the last disagreement that you had regarding an issue about which both you and the other person(s) felt strongly. How did you handle it?

_____

_____

2. Recall your most recent conflict that related to money or material possessions. How was it resolved?

_____

_____

3. Have you been affected by any serious disruption in your immediate family? Are you aware of serious disruptions in the immediate families of your co-workers or other acquaintances?

_____

_____

4. Have you or has anyone you know been involved in a legal conflict within the past year?

_____

_____

5. Which of your friends, co-workers, or family members have had to deal with alcohol or drug-related problems? What kinds of conflict did this cause?

_____

_____

6. Recall the last time you perceived someone meeting (or trying to meet) his or her needs at your expense. How did you handle the situation?

_____

_____

7. What are your personal "unthinkable" thoughts—the terrifying thoughts that sometimes wake you in the middle of the night?

_____

_____

8. Have you or has anyone close to you recently been in conflict with a public or private bureaucracy? How do you feel about the way large institutions are meeting your needs?

_____

_____

9. How many crimes or violent acts can you remember reading about, hearing about, or witnessing (live or on TV) during the past two weeks?

_____

_____

10. Recall the last time you had to wait in line, were trapped in traffic, were unable to get reservations, or had to fight crowds for any reason. How did it affect your disposition?

_____

_____

11. List as many social and environmental factors as you can think of that isolate you from more meaningful personal contact with others.

_____

_____

12. How are the communication media invading your mind and influencing your life?

_____

_____

Part 2

Ranking Personal Conflict Sources

1. The arguments, disruptions, and hassles in your life that cause you the most discomfort or pain are usually related to which of the following people? (Rank order these on the basis of how much pain and time they cost you. Use "1" for the category causing the most painful conflict and "10" for the category causing the least painful conflict.)

   _____ Spouse (or ex-spouse)

   _____ Parents

   _____ Children (or stepchildren)

   _____ Other relatives

   _____ Boss

   _____ Close friends

   _____ Co-workers

   _____ Subordinates

   _____ Clients

   Others:

   _____

   _____

2. Issues about which you feel strongly and about which you *most often* find yourself in conflict with others are related to which of the following topics? (Rank order these and add any others that are significant. Use "1" for the category that most often causes conflict.)

   _____ Money

   _____ Sexuality

   _____ Minority rights

   _____ Women's rights

   _____ General politics

   _____ Religion

   _____ Welfare

   _____ Legal System

   _____ Leisure

   _____ Drugs or alcohol

   _____ Smoking

   _____ Taxes

   _____ Gun Control

   _____ School integration

   _____ Divorce

   _____

Part 3

Personal Focus Sentence Completion

Write the first thoughts that enter your mind as you read the following sentences.

1. The greatest source of conflict for me in my family right now is ____

   _____

2. The greatest source of conflict for me in my job right now is _____

   _____

3. There would be less conflict in my life if _____

   _____

4. I am most likely to get into arguments when _____

   _____

5. The conflicts in my life over which I have the most control are ____

   _____

Part 4

Insights

1. Look over your responses to the first three parts of the survey. What insights have you gained?

   _____

   _____

   _____

   _____

2. Discuss your new insights with someone who knows you well. The payoff for this activity will be an awareness of how *you* fit into the change and conflict around you and how you feel about your situation. It provides another way to look inside yourself so that you can make better choices.

COMMENT

As the intensity and pervasiveness of conflict increases, so does our need for realistic personal awareness of its impact on our lives. To recognize the amount of energy we put into conflict-related behavior is only the first step in successful conflict management; the next step is to learn more about how we behave under pressure.

Chapter 2

Self-Awareness:
The Key to Conflict Management

I don't believe in anything or anyone; only in Zorba. Not because Zorba is better than the others; not at all, not a little bit! He's a brute like the rest! But I believe in Zorba because he's the only being I have in my power, the only one I know. All the rest are ghosts.

N. Kazantzakis
in Zorba the Greek

No one knows exactly how he or she will behave when faced with difficult interpersonal or intergroup confrontations, because rational responses are usually short-circuited by the stress of conflict. But the more a person learns about how he or she *might* react, the greater the chances for selecting the appropriate course of action. Unfortunately, this self-knowledge is extremely difficult to obtain. A self-help formula that promises to make people more assertive, lovable, and effective as they deal with conflict in their lives will not work if it does not fit the style of the person using it. To accept suggestions for handling conflict without spending some time on personal awareness and self-understanding is like buying mail order clothes—they will fit only if you are lucky. One must always ask, "Will this work for *me?*" Without understanding your potential as a conflict manager and examining your strengths, weaknesses, natural inclinations, and preferences, you will find limited value in "canned" suggestions, and they may even be detrimental.

The absence of self-awareness in conflict may cause you to be a victim of your limitations. You would be like a bull in the bullring—doomed by your own instinct and predictability. The matador, on the other hand, controls himself—as does any conflict manager—through a strong sense of self and an array of skills that fit his style. The matador adapts all of this to the unique situation he faces. The bull cannot adapt.

An understanding of the bullring analogy helps us avoid the most common and unproductive conflict management trap of all: *trying to change the other person.* This is almost impossible without using a powerful physical or psychological force. Even with force, the effect would be only temporary. Under normal conditions, most people tend to see what they want to see, hear what they want to hear, and do what they want to do; in conflicts, their positions become even more rigid and fixed. Yet for some unknown reason, we persist in believing that we can prevail and that the other person will see the light or by some miracle will come around to doing things our way. However, at the precise moment that we are trying so hard to change the other parties in the conflict, they are working just as hard to take care of themselves, and what they are doing may not have any relationship to our wants or needs.

Recognizing the limited possibilities of influencing another person under the stress of conflict can be very liberating, because it releases enormous amounts of energy to be used more productively in two ways: first, in learning to accept the other party and, second, in fully directing attention to *oneself,* which is the only variable in a conflict situation that a person can control.

Intellectually understanding all of this, however, is not enough. You could spend the rest of your life attending classes and lectures, reading self-help books, and following gurus, yet still be unable to manage conflict. True self-knowledge involves actively seeking out information about our innermost selves and then acting on what we learn. This is not easy. During conflict-management workshops, when the agenda provides for examining self and one's impact on others, participants become acutely uncomfortable. For those who push through the discomfort, however, the payoff is a more self-confident and hassle-free life style.

FOUR PATHWAYS TO INCREASED SELF-AWARENESS

Some people are "naturals" at handling conflict. They take it as it comes, intuitively doing and saying the right things and emerging unscathed from difficult and complex encounters. The first question is "How did they acquire this ability?" Intuitive intelligence, conditioning, and heredity contribute to it, but these people are keenly aware of their effect on other people. As a result of this awareness, they develop behavioral strategies that enable them to cope effectively when faced with opposition, hostility, and resistance. In other words, they "have their act together." The next logical question is "How can we obtain clear information and feedback about ourselves that will help us make better choices under pressure?" The answer can be found in one or more of the following pathways.

Pathway 1: Intrapersonal Awareness

When you are faced with conflict, there is usually a conversation going on inside of you. Pay attention to it. For example, the internal dialog may sound like this: "Mary is obviously angry with me. I'm feeling a little scared and I'll probably say something stupid, because I become tongue-tied when I feel like this." Be aware also of physical reactions: tight jaws? tense muscles? shaky voice?

Being in touch with yourself is a learnable skill requiring concentration and practice. Physical and emotional reactions to interpersonal situations are a rich source of clues. When these internal clues bubble up to your conscious level of awareness you are better able to choose an effective course of action. This skill is especially useful in conflict situations when emotions tend to override reason. People who kid themselves or mask their emotions tend to make mistakes when faced with conflict and opposition, because they are unaware of who they really are or what they are really feeling. If the person with whom you are in conflict knows more about your responses and can predict your behavior more accurately than you can, you are seriously handicapped, especially in emotionally charged situations.

The following activities will help you become more aware of your feelings:

- Practice listening to yourself during emotional moments without ignoring the feelings that make you uncomfortable (e.g., anger, fear, vengefulness, or hate). Realize that everyone has these emotions.

- Avoid lying to yourself or denying your true emotions, even if they are offensive to you. Remember the internal dialog is between you and you. No one else needs to know.

- The next time you are involved in a conflict, try to remain in touch with your true feelings. When it is over, review those feelings and ask yourself two questions: "Did I try to suppress or cover up how I felt in order to smooth things over or in order to look good?" and "What did I learn about myself that I can use the next time I'm in a similar situation?"

Pathway 2: Scanning Others for Clues About Ourselves

A personal "radar" system that accurately reads other people's reactions to your presence and your behavior is a necessary conflict-management tool. We are born with the intuitive capacity to use our sensors, but disuse or neglect erodes our natural ability and instead we develop protective postures that preserve the mental pictures of ourselves as we want to be or as we think we should be. Repossessing and fine-tuning your radar are not difficult tasks, and they can even be fun. Try a few of these suggestions:

- Become a keen observer of others as you relate to them. Concentrate on the emotions behind their words and look for subtle changes in voice, tone, facial expressions, and body language.

- Be alert at all times for verbal or nonverbal clues that may give you some news about yourself. Pay special attention to people who are not intimidated by you or who do not want something from you.

- Try to analyze reactions to your clothing, jewelry, hairstyle, and other symbols that make statements about who you are. Wear a color or style of clothing that you have not worn before and listen to the comments you receive. Push past the compliments to determine if the comment is a routine "stroke" or if you are genuinely being perceived differently. If it is the latter, you have learned that you are able to present a different image. In certain environments, clothes and other decor make a significant difference in the quality of human interaction.

- Practice behaving in different ways and observe the reaction. For example, speak a little louder or a little softer. Stand a little closer or a little farther away. Maintain longer eye contact. Experiment with behaviors that are not typical for you. You may receive some useful feedback and may choose to continue some of your new ways if the payoff seems worth it. Caution: These are not suggestions to try out *bizarre* behaviors, but rather to gradually move away from fixed ways of acting and reacting, thereby expanding your repertoire of behavioral options.

- Make a practice of people watching, especially during heated and emotional encounters. As you observe others, notice how they attend to each other and mentally place yourself in their positions and anticipate what will happen next. How many of your behaviors do you recognize in others? Do you like what you see?

- Pay close attention to the teasing you receive. Teasing almost always contains a trace of truth.
- Ask yourself the following questions and try to answer them honestly.

  1. Am I perceived differently at home than I am at work or other places?

  2. What do I believe people say about me when I'm not around (e.g., my family, friends, boss, subordinates, colleagues, and acquaintances)? Ask a few people what others say about you when you are not around. You may receive some surprising answers. Even if the answers do not surprise you, the reactions of those whom you ask will be interesting.

  3. How do others generally behave toward me when I show anger or other strong emotions?

  4. When faced with conflict or opposition, am I generally regarded as cool and controlled or high strung and intense?

  If you have any trouble answering these questions, be aware that you have lots of company. As you continue to scan others for information about yourself, the answers will come more easily.

Pathway 3: Seeking Feedback from Others and Practicing Self-Disclosure

Asking others to tell you about yourself may frighten you, but the benefits are well worth the risks. There is probably no better way to begin building interpersonal skills than to have people tell us as honestly as they can how we affect them. This kind of feedback keeps us from judging ourselves by our intentions while others judge us by our behavior. It is particularly important to discover how we affect people in emotionally charged situations—when our self-perception is often distorted.

Become involved in structured environments in which you can obtain formal feedback about your presence and style. Toastmaster organizations, public-speaking classes, personal-growth workshops, and communication seminars are available almost everywhere. In such settings—as you interact with others—you can learn how your feelings, as expresseed through your behavior, are perceived by others.

In the absence of available groups, ask a trusted person who knows you well to observe you in action at work or during recreation as you interact with others. Ask for honest feedback about how you are being perceived by others and try to accept what you hear without being too defensive. It is impossible to be totally nondefensive, but do the best you can. The reward is worth the pain as you begin to recognize the blind spots that make you vulnerable in conflict situations.

When no one else is available, observe yourself in the mirror. Ask yourself questions such as "How do I look as I am about to speak?" and "How do I look as I am speaking?" Check out your appearance. Listen to yourself on a tape recorder. Do you hear things on the playback that annoy you? If possible, watch yourself on videotape.

As you work on receiving feedback, practice a moderate amount of self-disclosure. Tell people how you feel without being aggressive or apologetic. Be a little more open with your thoughts than usual. Experiment with this behavior and develop some personal criteria about what is appropriate.[1]

A useful model (Figure 1), which can help bring you in touch with the personal value of feedback and self-disclosure, is the Johari Window (Hanson, 1973). The window is divided into four panes that represent four areas of knowledge about ourselves during interactions with others.

Pane 1 represents your open self—the public-knowledge area. In this pane, what others know about you corresponds with what you know about yourself. As this pane expands, communication becomes easier. Under conditions of conflict, however, this pane usually contracts because of fear of vulnerability.

Pane 2 represents blind spots: things others know about you that you do not know about yourself. This is sometimes referred to as the "bad-breath-and-dandruff" pane. A large Pane 2 increases your vulnerability under conflict and often makes you easy to manipulate. For example, if you are unaware of some mannerisms that aggravate others or that make you appear foolish, you are at a disadvantage. Accurate feedback can help you make better choices and shrink this pane.

Pane 3, your hidden self, contains things that you do not want others to know about you. Under conflict and conditions of low trust, this area becomes larger as you mask your feelings.

[1]"Appropriateness" may be defined as "fitting" or "suitable." Appropriate self-disclosure means the right kind and the right amount at the right time.

Pane 4 relates to information about you that neither you nor others know. Discovery in this section often occurs under conditions of extreme stress and conflict or when you are faced with situations never before encountered.

The configuration of each person's Johari Window is unique. Each pane expands and contracts according to the feedback we receive or the degree of self-disclosure we permit. By examining ourselves through this paradigm, we can increase our awareness and begin making choices about our interaction with others. As you study the configurations in Figure 2, contemplate the way your window compares with each of the four designs. Then spend some time answering the following questions:

How does your window look? Does it change when you are faced with conflict? How do you want it to be?

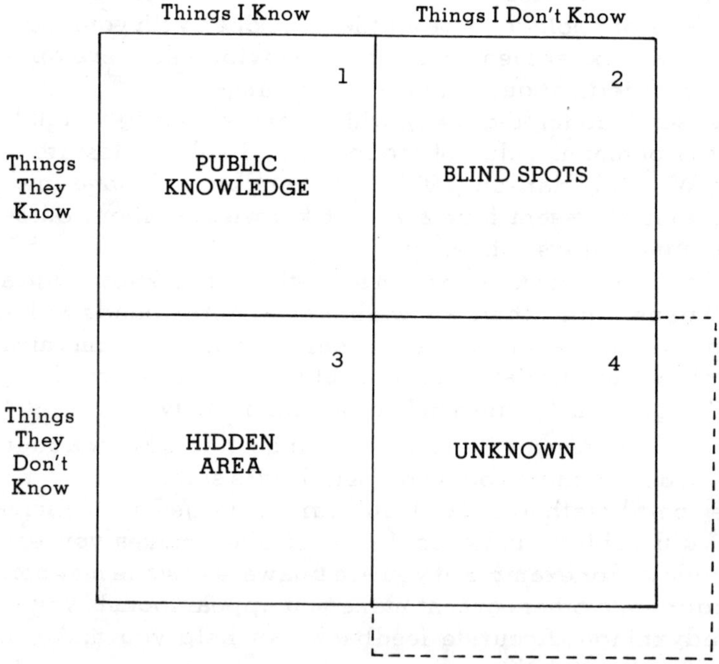

	Things I Know	Things I Don't Know
Things They Know	1 PUBLIC KNOWLEDGE	2 BLIND SPOTS
Things They Don't Know	3 HIDDEN AREA	4 UNKNOWN

Figure 1. The Johari Window Model

Adapted from: P.C. Hanson. The Johari Window: A Model for Soliciting and Giving Feedback. In J.E. Jones & J.W. Pfeiffer (Eds.), *The 1973 annual handbook for group facilitators.* San Diego, CA: University Associates, 1973. Used with permission.

As a step toward more information about yourself, complete the following sentences.

- I receive most feedback about myself from
  [name of person(s)]
  _____

  _____ .

- A person with whom I could be a little more open is _____

  _____ .

- The factors that prevent me from disclosing my true feelings to others are _____

  _____ .

- Under normal conditions I am probably perceived by most people as _____

  _____ .

- When I am faced with conflict, disagreement, or opposition I am probably perceived as _____

  _____ .

To learn more about feedback and self-disclosure read Powell (1969).

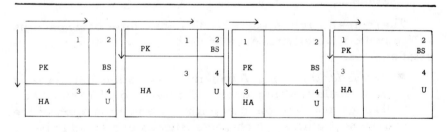

| Comfortably Open and Direct | Low in self-disclosure with a tendency to pin others down with questions | Inappropriately Open | Inappropriately Closed |

Figure 2. Various Configurations of the Johari Window

See footnote in Figure 1.

Pathway 4: Formal and Informal Behavioral Appraisal

The first three pathways to self-knowledge require significant
personal commitment, energy, and risks. A less demanding way
to learn about your behavior preferences and reactions is through
behavioral-science instruments. Measurement devices such as
scales, inventories, and evaluations can be useful in helping you
assess yourself and in predicting your behavior under a given set
of circumstances. Among the many formal instruments designed
by behavioral scientists, only a handful are of value in the area of
conflict management. Two of the most useful are the Strength
Deployment Inventory (SDI) by Porter (1973) and the Management
of Differences Exercise (MODE) by Thomas and Kilmann (1974).
After the following descriptions of these basic instruments, the full
text of the Conflict-Management Style Survey (CMSS) is given. It
will help you examine your own conflict-management style.

The Strength Deployment Inventory® consists of twenty
incomplete sentences, each with three possible endings. The
respondent distributes ten points among the three choices
according to behavioral preference in the given situation.

Sample Item.[2]

When I am at my best, I most enjoy . . .

seeing others benefit from what I have been able to do for them.	having others turn to me to lead and guide them and give them purpose.	being my own boss and doing things for myself and by myself.

The scores are interpreted as indicative of three basic patterns
of motivation underlying a person's behavior in interpersonal
relationships.

● *Altruistic/Nurturing.* A pattern of motivation that has as its
  most distinguishing quality the seeking of gratification
  through the promotion of harmony and promotion of the
  welfare of others and characteristically expressed in being
  trusting, optimistic, loyal, idealistic, helpful, modest, de-
  voted, caring, and supportive.

---

[2]Reprinted from: Strength Deployment Inventory®, Elias H. Porter,
Ph.D. Pacific Palisades, CA: Personal Strengths Publishing, Inc., 1973.
Used with permission. More information on the SDI and Porter's relation-
ship-awareness theory may be obtained from Personal Strengths Publishing, Inc., P.O. Drawer 397, Pacific Palisades, CA 92072-0397.

- *Assertive/Directing.* A pattern of motivation that has as its most distinguishing quality the seeking of gratification through self-assertion and through directing the activities of others and charcteristically expressed in being enterprising, self-confident, ambitious, persuasive, forceful, quick to act, imaginative, challenging, proud, bold, and risk taking.
- *Analytic/Autonomizing.* A pattern of motivation that has as its most distinguishing quality the seeking of gratification through the achievement of self-sufficiency, self-reliance, and logical orderliness and characteristically expressed in being cautious, practical, economical, reserved, methodical, principled, orderly, fair, preserving, conserving, and thorough.

The SDI is a positively focused and nonthreatening instrument that enables a person to assess the way he or she deploys strengths in conflict situations and to contrast it with the way strengths are deployed when things are going well. It takes fifteen to twenty minutes to administer and ten to fifteen minutes to score.

The Conflict Mode Instrument[3] is an easily administered, self-scoring set of thirty items, each with two alternatives. The instrument measures a person's relative use of five conflict-handling modes in situations in which his or her wishes differ from those of another person.

Sample Items.

A. I try to postpone the issue until I have had some time to think it over.
B. I give up some points in exchange for others.

A. I am usually firm in pursuing my goals.
B. I might try to soothe the other's feelings and preserve our relationship.

A scale or graph is developed for measuring preferences for competing, accommodating, avoiding, compromising, or collaborating.

The Mode takes ten to fifteen minutes to administer and five to ten minutes to score.

The Conflict-Management Style Survey (CMSS) will help you to assess your style of response to everyday conflict situations. The complete instrument is included.

---

[3]The instrument and manual may be ordered from: Xicom, Inc., Sterling Forest, Tuxedo, NY 10987.

CONFLICT-MANAGEMENT STYLE SURVEY[4]

Instructions: Choose a single frame of reference for answering all fifteen items (e.g., work-related conflicts, family conflicts, or social conflicts) and keep that frame of reference in mind when answering the items.

Allocate 10 points among the four alternative answers given for each of the fifteen items below.

Example: When the people I supervise become involved in a personal conflict, I usually:

Intervene to settle the dispute.	Call a meeting to talk over the problem.	Offer to help if I can.	Ignore the problem.
3	6	1	0

Be certain that your answers add up to 10.

1. When someone *I care about* is actively hostile toward me, i.e., yelling, threatening, abusive, etc., I tend to:

Respond in a hostile manner.	Try to persuade the person to give up his/her actively hostile behavior.	Stay and listen as long as possible.	Walk away.
_____	_____	_____	_____

2. When someone *who is relatively unimportant to me* is actively hostile toward me, i.e., yelling, threatening, abusive, etc., I tend to:

Respond in a hostile manner.	Try to persuade the person to give up his/her actively hostile behavior.	Stay and listen as long as possible.	Walk away.
_____	_____	_____	_____

[4]Reprinted from: M. Robert. Conflict-Management Style Survey. In J.W. Pfeiffer & L.D. Goodstein (Eds.), *The 1982 Annual for Facilitators, Trainers, and Consultants.* San Diego, CA: University Associates, 1982. Used with permission.

3. When I observe people in conflicts in which anger, threats, hostility, and strong opinions are present, I tend to:

Become involved and take a position.	Attempt to mediate.	Observe to see what happens.	Leave as quickly as possible.
_____	_____	_____	_____

4. When I perceive another person as meeting his/her needs at my expense, I am apt to:

Work to do anything I can to change that person.	Rely on persuasion and "facts" when attempting to have that person change.	Work hard at changing how I relate to that person.	Accept the situation as it is.
_____	_____	_____	_____

5. When involved in an interpersonal dispute, my general pattern is to:

Draw the other person into seeing the problem as I do.	Examine the issues between us as logically as possible.	Look hard for a workable compromise.	Let time take its course and let the problem work itself out.
_____	_____	_____	_____

6. The quality that I value the most in dealing with conflict would be:

Emotional strength and security.	Intelligence.	Love and openness.	Patience.
_____	_____	_____	_____

7. Following a serious altercation with someone I care for deeply, I:

Strongly desire to go back and settle things my way.	Want to go back and work it out—whatever give-and-take is necessary.	Worry about it a lot but not plan to initiate further contact.	Let it lie and not plan to initiate further contact.
_____	_____	_____	_____

8. When I see a serious conflict developing between two people *I care about,* I tend to:

Express my disappointment that this had to happen.	Attempt to persuade them to resolve their differences.	Watch to see what develops.	Leave the scene.
_____	_____	_____	_____

9. When I see a serious conflict developing between two people who are *relatively unimportant to me,* I tend to:

Express my disappointment that this had to happen.	Attempt to persuade them to resolve their differences.	Watch to see what develops.	Leave the scene.
_____	_____	_____	_____

10. The feedback that I receive from most people about how I behave when faced with conflict and opposition indicates that I:

Try hard to get my way.	Try to work out differences cooperatively.	Am easygoing and take a soft or conciliatory position.	Usually avoid the conflict.
_____	_____	_____	_____

11. When communicating with someone with whom I am having a serious conflict, I:

Try to over-power the other person with my speech.	Talk a little bit more than I listen.	Am an active listener (feeding back words and feelings).	Am a passive listener (agreeing and apologizing).
_____	_____	_____	_____

12. When involved in an unpleasant conflict, I:

Use humor with the other party.	Make an occasional quip or joke about the situation or the relationship.	Relate humor only to myself.	Suppress all attempts at humor.
_____	_____	_____	_____

13. When someone does something that irritates me (e.g., smokes in a nonsmoking area or crowds in line in front of me), my tendency in communicating with the offending person is to:

Insist that the person look me in the eye.	Look the person directly in the eye and maintain eye contact.	Maintain intermittent eye contact.	Avoid looking directly at the person.
_____	_____	_____	_____

14.
Stand close and make physical contact.	Use my hands and body to illustrate my points.	Stand close to the person without touching him or her.	Stand back and keep my hands to myself.
_____	_____	_____	_____

15.
Use strong, direct language and tell the person to stop.	Try to persuade the person to stop.	Talk gently and tell the person what my feelings are.	Say and do nothing.
_____	_____	_____	_____

CONFLICT-MANAGEMENT STYLE SURVEY
SCORING AND INTERPRETATION SHEET

Instructions: When you have completed all fifteen items, add your scores vertically, resulting in four column totals. Put these on the blanks below.

Totals: _____   _____   _____   _____
          Column 1   Column 2   Column 3   Column 4

    Using your total scores in each column, fill in the bar graph below.

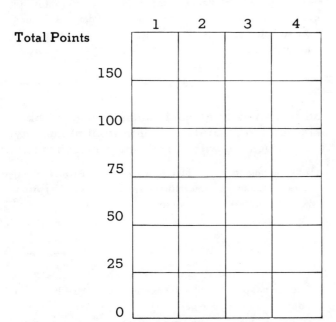

Column 1. Aggressive/Confrontive. High scores indicate a tendency toward "taking the bull by the horns" and a strong need to control situations and/or people. Those who use this style are often directive and judgmental.

Column 2. Assertive/Persuasive. High scores indicate a tendency to stand up for oneself without being pushy, a proactive approach to conflict, and a willingness to collaborate. People who use this style depend heavily on their verbal skills.

Column 3. Observant/Introspective. High scores indicate a tendency to observe others and examine oneself analytically in response to conflict situations as well as a need to adopt counseling and listening modes of behavior. Those who use this style are likely to be cooperative, even conciliatory.

Column 4. Avoiding/Reactive. High scores indicate a tendency toward passivity or withdrawal in conflict situations and a need to avoid confrontation. Those who use this style are usually accepting and patient, often suppressing their strong feelings.

Now total your scores for Columns 1 and 2 and Columns 3 and 4.

                                          Score
Column 1 + Column 2 = _____ A
Column 3 + Column 4 = _____ B

If Score A is significantly higher than Score B (25 points or more), it may indicate a tendency toward aggressive/assertive conflict management. A significantly higher B score signals a more conciliatory approach.

Do these interpretations give you any insights? Do they fit you? Are any changes desired? Write your comments below.

_____

_____

_____

_____

CONFLICT-MANAGEMENT STYLE SURVEY REACTION ACTIVITY

1. Discuss with someone the following questions in the light of your scores on the Conflict-Management Style Survey.

- Are you aware of impending conflicts? Can you easily tell when "all hell is about to break loose?"
- Do you communicate (i.e., send and receive) differently in conflicts than you do normally?

- Which of your emotions generally surface during conflict or opposition?
- Compare your scores on items 1 and 2 of the Conflict-Management Style Survey. Do they differ? Repeat for items 8 and 9.
- Which items gave you the most difficulty in answering?

2. Compare your scores with the scores of those with whom you live and/or work. Where are the variances? Discuss the differences and similarities. Where are possible trouble spots? How would you assess compatibility? Can a high A-score person work well with another high A-score person? What are some mutual insights?

3. Ask someone who knows you well to fill out a blank copy of the CMSS in a way that reflects how they perceive you. Compare and contrast the scores with your own. Discuss the differences. What is your insight?

Less formal but equally successful instruments may be developed spontaneously to raise people's awareness of their beliefs, attitudes, and behaviors. Such devices can simply be in the form of questions, checklists, scales, or sentence stems, such as those on preceding pages. For example, the following Conflict-Management Dialog is a simple sentence-completion activity that was converted into an informal instrument for the purpose of raising interpersonal-conflict awareness.

Although the complete instrument is presented for use by management or human-relations trainers, it can easily be adapted for general use in home or office by any two people. Simply copy each item on a separate card and follow the directions. This dialog has been a successful team-building activity, particularly among workers in high intensity, people-related jobs.

CONFLICT MANAGEMENT: DYADIC SHARING[5]

Goals

    I. To identify and share reactions to ways of dealing with conflict.

    II. To explore new ideas about managing conflict.

[5]Adapted from: M. Robert. Conflict Management: Dyadic Sharing. In J.E. Jones & J.W. Pfeiffer (Eds.), *The 1979 Annual Handbook for Group Facilitators*. San Diego, CA: University Associates, 1979. Used with permission.

Group Size

An unlimited number of dyads (paired partners).

Materials Required

    I. A Conflict-Management Booklet for each participant. (The booklet should be prepared in such a way that participants are presented statements one at a time.)

    II. Newsprint and a felt-tipped marker.

Physical Setting

A room large enough for the dyads to converse without disturbing one another.

Process

    I. The activity is introduced by stating that everyone is involved in some type of conflict at one time or other and that most people have evolved their own methods of dealing with conflict. By sharing and discussing these methods, we can identify conflict-management techniques from which all can benefit.

    II. The participants are directed to regroup in pairs and each is given a copy of the Conflict-Management Booklet.

    III. The participants are told that they are to take turns responding to or completing each statement in the booklet and that they are not to look ahead in the booklet, but are to proceed from one page to another. They will have a half-hour in which to complete the activity.

    IV. The total group is reassembled, and participants are encouraged to share what they learned about their methods of dealing with conflict.

    V. Participants then discuss what new ways of viewing or managing conflict they learned from each other as a result of the sharing process. Pertinent learnings may be listed on newsprint. The group is encouraged to discuss situations in which these learnings and techniques could be applied.

Variations

    I. Each partner can complete each statement, alternating who goes first.

    II. Again in pairs, the participants can role play a conflict situation for each member, utilizing the skills they just learned.

    III. Participants can fill out the personal parts of the booklet, meet in small groups, and share and discuss those items most relevant to each group.

Conflict-Management Booklet

Prior to the experience, a booklet should be prepared for each participant. The booklet will begin with page 1 and will be prepared in such a way that participants see only one page at a time. The contents of the booklet are as follows:

. . . .

CONFLICT MANAGEMENT: DYADIC SHARING   1

. . . .

Read silently. Do not look ahead in the booklet, because the   2
experience is effective only if your answers are spontaneous
and unrehearsed.

This booklet contains a series of open-ended statements
intended to help you discover and share your reactions to
conflict and your ways of dealing with it. You also will have
an opportunity to learn from your partner's responses.

The ground rules to be followed:

1. Take turns initiating the discussion. Complete each
   statement orally. (Do not write in the booklet.)

2. This discussion is *confidential.*

3. Do not look ahead in the booklet.

4. Do not skip items. Respond to each one in the order
   in which it appears.

When both you and your partner have finished reading
this page, you may turn the page and begin.

. . . .

Conflict is . . .   3

. . . .

The time I felt best about dealing with conflict was when . . .   4

. . . .

When someone disagrees with me about something im- 5
portant or challenges me in front of others, I usually . . .

. . . .

When I get angry, I . . . 6

. . . .

When I think of negotiating, I . . . 7

. . . .

The most important outcome of conflict is . . . 8

. . . .

I usually react to negative criticism by . . . 9

. . . .

When I confront someone I care about, I . . . 10

. . . .

I feel most vulnerable during a conflict when . . . 11

. . . .

I resent . . . 12

. . . .

When someone avoids conflict with me, I . . . 13

. . . .

My greatest strength in handling conflict is . . . 14

. . . .

Right now I am feeling . . .   15

. . . .

Here is an actual situation in which I was involved in a   16
conflict (*explain*). What do you think I did? How do you
think I felt?

(*Tell your partner how accurate his or her prediction is.*)

. . . .

When things are not going well I tend to . . .   17

. . . .

I imagine that you handle most conflicts by . . .   18
(*Check out your prediction with your partner.*)

. . . .

I will sometimes avoid unpleasant situations by   19
(*explain*) . . .

. . . .

I am most apt to confront people in situations such as . . .   20

. . . .

I usually hide or camouflage my feelings when . . .   21

. . . .

My greatest weakness in handling conflict is . . .   22

. . . .

When I think about confronting a potentially unpleasant   23
person, I . . .

. . . .

I sometimes avoid directly confronting someone when . . .   24

. . . .

I am most likely to assert myself in situations that . . .   25

. . . .

With you and me, conflict could . . .   26

. . . .

By next year I would like to be able to handle conflict better   27
by improving my ability to . . .

. . . .

Completing and scoring an instrument is only the beginning. The true value of the activity is in the interpretation and discussion of the results. The least that the instrument should do is to heighten your awareness of yourself at a given point in time. At best, it should provide you with a powerful incentive to change certain unproductive behavior.

The usefulness of an instrument may be enhanced by "shadowing," a process wherein you give a blank copy of an instrument that you have completed to someone who knows you well. The person is instructed to fill it out in a way that reflects how he or she perceives you. Then compare the scores and discuss the interpretations with that person.

This discussion of instruments is intended only to suggest another way of learning about yourself. Pfeiffer, Heslin, and Jones (1976) provide some excellent information on instrumentation and describe numerous instruments for human relations training. They also provide information for ordering the instruments.

COMMENT

Specific ways have been suggested for getting in touch with your internal world in order to develop a clear sense of who you are and what you need, because what is inside of you has such a profound influence on your encounters with others that no effective system of interpersonal-conflict management can be developed without some serious introspection. It takes energy, discipline, and commitment to follow the personal-awareness paths described in this chapter, but the payoff should be worth the effort as you begin reacting with more personal power to life's conflicts.

Although programs, systems, and gimmicks to ease the pain of conflict will always be available, even the most consistently effective practices can be botched by people who are out of touch with themselves. The chapters that follow will provide a smorgasbord of ideas, activities, and check lists for learning to avoid, prevent, and handle conflicts and to take good care of yourself in the process. The more accurately you perceive yourself, the more effectively you will be able to take advantage of the "how tos" that comprise the rest of the book.

Chapter 3

How To Avoid Becoming Embroiled
in Unproductive Conflict

God grant me the serenity
To accept the things I cannot change,
Courage to change the things I can,
And wisdom to know the difference.

A.A. Prayer

Chapter 2 dealt primarily with our private inner space as it relates to conflict. Chapter 3 moves us outside ourselves into the arena of potential interpersonal and intergroup conflict, where *our* perceptions of reality bump into those of *others.* We will explore this arena to learn how and when to prevent some of the useless conflicts that visit us daily.

We all know people who seem to spend their lives embroiled and embattled. They argue with their friends and families, berate their subordinates, and seem unable to get along with their bosses and co-workers. We refer to such people with many kinds of negative words: hard nosed, opinionated, mean spirited, pain in the neck, S.O.B., and worse. However, all of them are probably doing exactly what they need to do, given their perceptions of reality. What they lack are the insight and skills needed to avoid and prevent unproductive conflict.[6]

Although a certain amount of conflict is useful in clarifying issues, strengthening relationships, solving problems, and otherwise enriching our lives, sometimes conflict is not only unproductive but also destructive. Furthermore, it is often avoidable or preventable. Most unwarranted conflict is attracted and aggravated by assumptions, wrong judgments about one's own motives, inappropriate behavior, or countless other human mistakes. The

---

[6]In this context, conflict is "unproductive" if it is physically, emotionally, or socially destructive to one or more of the parties.

art of effective conflict management includes learning how to avoid such mistakes.

This chapter will assist you in avoiding the avoidable and in the prevention of unnecessary escalation. Sometimes you will be able to *avoid* conflict by *not* doing anything to contribute to or aggravate it. At other times you can *prevent* conflict by *active* participation in the relationship. In either case, the results are the same: You have learned to recognize potential conflict and behave in a manner that makes the conflict unnecessary.

The focus of this chapter is again on heightening your self-awareness. You will try to discover what you are doing that contributes to your involvement in unnecessary conflict that is unpleasant or destructive. The chapter contains nine sections, and some of these provide check lists to help clarify your options and values. The renegotiation model in the last section offers a system for staying out of trouble rather than getting out of trouble.

1. KNOW THE DIFFERENCE BETWEEN YOUR PRINCIPLES AND YOUR PREFERENCES

Many of us are drawn into senseless arguments over trivial issues. Friendships are destroyed, marriages are jeopardized, and people are killed in conflicts that erupted because someone was unable to stop the momentum of anger and ask himself or herself, "How important is this in my life?"

Without a clear set of personal priorities and values to live by we are guaranteed the prospect of continually being drawn into conflict over insignificant issues. On the other hand, when you possess some clearly defined bottom lines that say "I will go this far and no farther," you become predictable and less vulnerable to being misjudged by others. Being clear with yourself and significant others about your basic values will not only keep you out of much unwarranted conflict, but it will help build more trusting relationships.

A friend of mine is rarely involved in serious conflicts in spite of a very vulnerable job in an unusually contentious work environment. When I asked him what his secret was, he said, "I can't afford to sweat the small stuff. I choose my conflicts very carefully." He obviously has made some clear distinctions between his principles and preferences, and he avoids being drawn into conflict over low level preferences. The following work sheet will help you sort out some of your principles and preferences.

Conflict Values Self-Check

1. Are you clear about what values you will not compromise (i.e., issues over which you would risk almost anything)? What are your bottom-line items at work? at home? in general?

_____

_____

_____

2. What kinds of issues and situations draw you into conflict with others at work? at home? in general? Are these situations or issues worth the trouble?

_____

_____

_____

3. According to your value system, can you differentiate betweeen high level principles and low level preferences? If you have doubts, look at the following items in terms of how much energy you would give them.

   ● Your co-worker continually smokes in the work area you share. The smoke causes you discomfort. Your co-worker is otherwise compatible.
   You would: _____

_____

_____

- You are asked by your supervisor to participate in what you think amounts to bribing a government official in order to assure a contract.
  You would: _____

  _____

  _____

- You share a new product design idea with your closest friend at work. He presents it to your unit manager and takes full credit.
  You would: _____

  _____

  _____

- Your best friend defaults on a loan for which you co-signed.
  You would: _____

  _____

  _____

- Your supervisor asks you to be an accomplice in a cover-up for a current extramarital affair, i.e., you would have to provide your supervisor's spouse with false information to corroborate the cover-up story.
  You would: _____

  _____

  _____

- Your subordinates are using language you do not approve of. They are also telling racist jokes.
  You would: _____

  _____

  _____

- Your subordinates are obviously pilfering office supplies from your unit, but not enough to significantly impinge on company profits. They are otherwise working well.
  You would: _____

  _____

  _____

- Your sixteen-year-old daughter announces that she is going camping (unchaperoned) for the weekend with her boyfriend and another teen-age couple.
  You would: _____

  _____

  _____

Talking to yourself about these kinds of situations will help you clarify basic values and make better choices about becoming involved in conflicts over issues that are important to you and avoiding the other kind. For additional help in value clarification, see Keyes (1973), Kirschenbaum (1977), Simon, Howe, and Kirschenbaum (1972), and Smith (1977).

2. REALITY TEST YOUR EXPECTATIONS

Whenever we expect more of others than they are prepared to give, we run the risk of unwarranted conflict. Unrealistic expectations for children, unrealistic hopes that spouses will change, and unrealistic beliefs that—given enough time—inefficient employees will improve are examples of the proclivity to want things to be what they may never be.

Although high standards and optimism are commendable, trouble often occurs when we either do not recognize or cannot accept what is real. When it becomes clear that our children, spouses, employees, or others are not going to behave according to our expectations, we experience conflict and its by-products— disappointment, frustration, and anger. Driven by these emotions, we either push harder or express resentment—two courses of action that are rarely productive.

When you catch yourself hoping that someone will behave in a certain way, it may be possible to avoid useless conflict by testing your expectations against any of the following questions that are appropriate to the situation:

- What is wrong with the way the person is behaving? How is it affecting you? (The problem may be yours.)
- How long has the person been behaving this way? (The longer it has been going on, the less likelihood of a change.)
- Do I know specifically how I want the person to change? (Try not to generalize.)
- Is the person capable of changing? (He or she may not have the necessary physical, mental, and emotional resources.)
- What would be the reward for changing? (Without some perceived payoff, no one does anything.)
- Can I adapt to the situation or is it totally unacceptable? (If you cannot adapt, you should consider your options.)

For more on handling conflicts as problems to be solved, see Chapter 5.

3. PRACTICE SAVING AND SPENDING TRUST CREDITS

According to Selye (1974), it is not always possible to "love thy neighbor as thyself," but one can work on "earning thy neighbor's love." Although this advice seems at first glance to be a Pollyanna prescription, further examination reveals some real and practical value for the prevention of conflict.

In most human relationships, there is considerable give and take as people take small risks with each other over long periods of time. As these interactions develop, accounts of trust and credibility credits are built up in a variety of ways. How these credits are saved and spent can make a significant difference when relationships become strained or threatened. A person's attitude toward trust will determine how a relationship develops. People can take the position "I will not trust you until you prove to me that you can be trusted" or "I will trust you until you show me that I should do otherwise." Because it is almost impossible to predict another person's trust position, a positive and safe course of action is to spend some time each day consciously building good will through thoughtful and considerate behavior toward friends, family, colleagues, and acquaintances.

Continually ask yourself questions such as: "Will what I am about to do help this relationship or hurt it?" "Will it make others feel good or bad?" and "Will I appear dependable?" Conducting this internal dialog and acting on it is the way to build trust credits. The more consistently this is practiced, the faster the account will grow. Under certain conditions it is possible to build trust by asking for help, because the helper will invest in the relationship and both parties will establish a credit exchange.

An example of the need for trust building is found in the increasing numbers of women, ethnic minorities, older people, and the handicapped introduced into the work force to meet Equal Employment Opportunity hiring goals. These workers often encounter resentment and hostility and experience considerable difficulty. The more aware, creative, and sensitive employees usually develop systems of rapidly building trust and credibility, thereby blending smoothly into the work force and avoiding much unnecessary conflict.

We are far less vulnerable to conflict when we have deposited some trust credits in a relationship, because in a pinch we can call in some of our chips. We have all done this. For example, if I have handled a number of unpleasant tasks and done a series of favors for a friend or colleague and later make some demands on his time and energy, he will be less likely to refuse or to resent my request because he "owes me one" and the equation of trust is beginning to balance.

Hatfield and Walster (1978) make some sobering but realistic points regarding the equity theory and love:[7]

> Society consists of a collection of selfish people. If society is to survive, its members must learn to compromise. They must accept the

---

[7]Reprinted from: *A New Look at Love* by Elaine Hatfield and G. William Walster. Copyright © 1978 by Elaine Hatfield and G. William Walster. Used by permission of Addison-Wesley Publishing Company.

notion that you have to give a little to get a little, and that the more you give, the more you can expect to get.

People feel most comfortable when they're getting exactly what they feel they deserve in a relationship. Everyone in an inequitable relationship feels uneasy. While it's not surprising that deprived partners (who are, after all, getting less than they deserve) should feel resentful and angry about their inequitable treatment, it's perhaps not so obvious why their overbenefited mates (who are getting more than they deserve) feel uneasy too. But they do. They feel guilty and fearful of losing their favored position.

Men and women who discover that they're in an inequitable relationship attempt to eliminate their mutual distress by restoring equity. They generally go about this in one of three ways:

- They try to restore actual equity to their relationship.
- They try to restore psychological equity to their relationship. (They try to convince themselves and others that their obviously inequitable relationship really is "perfectly fair.")
- They also simply decide to end their relationship. (p. 135)

It is essential, then, not only to work at earning the love, respect, and good will of others but to allow others to work at earning yours. To be owed too much may be just as destructive as to owe excessively. Both conditions produce resentment. When trust accounts in work, recreation, or love relationships get out of balance, the potential for unproductive conflict increases. This point is especially applicable in organizations, because unbalanced trust accounts can cause both employees and managers who feel used or abused to display passive-aggressive behavior. Increased dysfunction can also be expected from workers who feel underproductive and overcompensated. In any case, the results of these imbalances will ultimately be more useless conflict and a less-effective work force.

Self-Check.

- Did you build any trust credits with anyone this week?
- Did you ask anyone for anything that might have been resented?
- With whom is your trust account in the best balance? The most out of balance?
- How do you handle it when you feel that someone "owes" you?
- To whom do you feel you "owe" the most? How does it feel?

4. HANDLE CRITICISM AS YOU WOULD A LIVE BOMB

As a species we have not evolved enough to accept criticism graciously. This opinion has been validated many times through personal and professional experience and by countless authorities. Recently a group of prominent behavioral scientists was asked to react in a word or phrase to the concept "criticism." Here are some of their responses.

Criticism:

- Never feels good;
- Is rarely helpful;
- Usually doesn't work;
- Irritates, aggravates, and sometimes enrages;
- Makes people self-conscious and defensive;
- Precipitates interpersonal conflicts; and
- Is almost always handled clumsily.

Most of the other comments were in the same vein. Only a small percentage of criticism is seriously listened to, and even less is positively accepted or acted on. The reason is simple: No one wants to hear bad news about himself or herself. Unfortunately the world is filled with people who feel compelled to tell others about their shortcomings. This would not be so bad except that pointing out deficiencies requires a degree of skill and judgment not possessed by most. With considerable training one can learn how to criticize in ways that minimize tension and promote growth, but it takes effort, practice, and natural sensitivity. Reading may help, and some excellent resources are available (e.g., Gordon, 1970; Simon, 1978). Reading and knowing about criticism, however, cannot replace more productive behavior. In the interest of preventing unproductive confrontations, the following ideas are offered as *alternatives* to criticism.

1. Take a moment to examine your intent before you criticize. Ask yourself what you will gain from it and what you stand to lose.
2. Study the recipient of your potential criticism. Is he or she hassled, upset, feeling low, or off balance? How is this person likely to respond?
3. Consider modeling the change you would like to see in the other person. For example, if the person is too talkative, try talking less. If he or she is habitually late, be punctual.

Sometimes people notice these things and recognize their own faults.

4. Describe behavior or situations *without* a value judgment. For example, say, "It's time to leave now" instead of "Aren't you ready yet?" "Your voice is becoming louder" instead of "Why must you always yell?" There is a considerable difference between an observation and an attack.

5. Be patient. Curb your impulse to criticize for at least five minutes. The feeling may go away or the situation may correct itself.

6. Finally, if you must criticize someone, do it in a kind and caring way that shows you put some time and energy into the positive suggestions that you are making.

Criticizing others, like any other habit, is difficult to break unless the person is rewarded for stopping. Some of the payoffs for withholding criticism are time saved, energy more productively redirected, and less unnecessary interpersonal conflict.

Self-Check.

- Do you tend to criticize openly or subtly?
- Are you aware of how you criticize nonverbally?
- Does your style of criticism produce the results you want?
- When was the last time your criticism produced a desired change in another person?
- Is it easy or difficult for you to handle negative criticism directed toward you?
- Thinking about your own style and needs (as in Chapter 2) and considering what you have read thus far, would you be willing to practice some alternatives to criticism?

5. PRACTICE THE POWER OF OPTIMISM

In 1964, *Saturday Review* editor Norman Cousins cured himself of the rare and crippling collagen disease, ankylosing spondylitis.[8] With the cooperation of his doctor, he moved out of the hospital, stopped taking all drugs, prescribed for himself massive doses of Vitamin C, and literally laughed himself back to good health by

[8]Doctors are unable to explain this recovery just as they are unable to explain many other mind-induced cures. Cousins is currently working with the UCLA Medical School to learn more about the effects of positive emotions on the human body. For details see Cousins (1979).

viewing Marx Brothers' movies and segments of old Candid Camera television shows. This remarkable case is perhaps the best known of the thousands that comprise a burgeoning body of evidence scientifically validating the tremendous power of the mind in influencing our physiology and our interpersonal environment.

Tiger (1979) states that optimism is a basic element of human survival for which we may be genetically programed.[9]

> What are the tangible consequences of optimistic thoughts? One consequence is that optimists seem more likely to cope and reproduce than pessimists. Because happy thoughts make us feel good, we want to spread their power, even onto the next generation. Cortical events which comprise optimistic thoughts, produce general feelings of well-being elsewhere in the bodily system just as sad thoughts can make us feel bad in our bodies and even prove to be fatal. (p.25)

From Tiger, Cousins, and many distinguished medical, behavioral, and social scientists, comes compelling evidence that *what you think is what you get.* Just as the mind produces biochemical changes in the body, it is capable of consistently and powerfully influencing interpersonal relationships. Personal observations convince me each day that people who approach life with positive expectations and who assume that things will turn out well rather than badly seem to attract significantly less unwarranted conflict than do those inclined toward cynicism and pessimism. Furthermore, optimists tend either to manage or to transcend unavoidable conflicts more effectively. Anyone who wishes to can learn to approach life in more positive ways. The following three steps may help you to program yourself to reduce unnecessary conflict in your life.

Step I: Observation

Constantly and carefully observe the behavior of friends, family members, and colleagues who appear cheerful and well disposed most of the time. Study the ways in which they approach or avoid conflict situations. Make mental notes regarding behaviors that work for them and that might also fit your style and value system. Experiment with a few of these behaviors and continue to study successful and happy people.

---

[9]Reprinted from: L. Tiger. Optimism: The Biological Roots of Hope. *Psychology Today* Magazine, January 1979. Copyright © 1979, Ziff Davis Publishing Co. Used with permission.

Step II: Practice

Try to maintain an *almost* naive optimism about the way circumstances will turn out. Assume that most people with whom you are in conflict probably want to stop hurting just as much as you do. Exaggerate this attitude and stop just short of being Pollyannaish. You may have to force this behavior for a while because the prevailing mood is one of fashionable cynicism. Nevertheless, an optimistic posture helps you develop good will, which contributes to a calm and tension-free environment, in which unnecessary conflict cannot thrive. This is *not* a suggestion to become a nonassertive doormat or to take abuse.

Step III: Turnabout

Get off the cynicism circuit. Although some complaining, carping, and wallowing are normal and sometimes useful modes of human expression, conflict and dissatisfaction almost always become the norm when one constantly feeds on a diet of depressing news and catastrophic expectations. Cynicism becomes first a game and then a habit that can poison relationships and paralyze positive action.

When you find yourself in the company of "ain't-it-awful," "what-if," and "moaning-and-groaning" game players, work at changing the focus to "what can we do about this?" If there is no positive reaction, walk away temporarily to preserve your own mental health. You may be able to help at a later time when the climate changes or when things become so bad that people are willing to take positive action.

Perceiving life optimistically and being around people of like persuasion help us retain hope, live longer, and feel better. For some people this is quite a departure from the norm and can be very difficult to do. Nevertheless, the evidence is convincing: A consistently positive mental attitude will help us reduce unwarranted conflict and manage unavoidable conflict more effectively.

Self-Check.

- Who are the most optimistic people in your life, the ones around whom you almost always feel good? Write their names here: _____

_____

How much time do you spend with them? ————————

● Who are the people in your life who bring you down, upset you, or are otherwise toxic to your well-being?[10] Write their names here: ————————————————————

————————————————————————————

How do you deal with them? ————————————

————————————————————————————

● Do you tend to be optimistic about the outcome of difficult and unknown situations, problems, or events, or do you often torture yourself with catastrophic expectations? Answer honestly and then, for homework, ask a few friends how they perceive your optimism/pessimism ratio.

6. BE AWARE OF PERSONAL GROWTH HAZARDS

Schur (1977) explores the seductiveness of the human-potential movement and its impact on our society. The current craze—intensified by the media—for awareness and self-help has, according to Schur, invited us to become preoccupied with ourselves and our sensations. "It is diluting our already weak feelings of social responsibility. And ironically in its approach to 'relationships' it may be encouraging manipulative behavior of precisely the sort it claims to abhor" (p. 7).

Schur's thesis points out a troublesome dilemma related to interpersonal conflict. Our pursuit of knowledge about ourselves for the purpose of improving our relationships may put us so far "into ourselves" that we inhibit our sensitivity to the pain and the needs of others. This self-preoccupation may precipitate unwarranted conflict as our sense of social responsibility becomes dulled. Unfortunately, it can happen insidiously.

An antidote may be found in realistically examining what is happening in your life and becoming aware, not only of your needs, but of the responsibilities of living among others. As a

———————————

[10]For more information about toxic relationships and how to deal with them, read Greenwald (1973).

colleague put it, "While all these people are out getting their consciousness raised, who's minding the store?"

Harvard research psychiatrist Robert Coles (1981) puts it another way, describing the proliferation of sensitivity and personal growth groups: "All these hucksters who tell us what to think and feel, try to make us cool and collected . . . . and what is the result? An everrising incident of malignant self-centeredness. The endless dwelling on one's own feelings and fantasies characterizes too much of the population that's called privileged in this society."

If you discover that you are crossing the line from self-awareness to self-preoccupation, examine the following questions and answer them as honestly as you can. Interpret the questions any way you wish and answer each one with a simple yes or no.

1. Have you recently (within the past six months) participated in a personal-growth or self-awareness experience that was stimulating and exhilarating?
2. If so, did you have difficulty discussing your exhilaration? Did you choose not to discuss these feelings with significant others in your life?
3. Are you often resentful of taking care of others' needs before taking care of your own?
4. Is it sometimes difficult to listen to people with views different from yours?
5. Do many other people seem less aware than you are of the "important" things in life?
6. Do others seem to "turn off" when you talk about your growth needs, experiences, and feelings?
7. Do you frequently feel as though you have missed out on a lot in life and need to make up for lost time?
8. Are you envious of some of the things people "get away" with?
9. Do you spend much time thinking about ways to make significant changes in your life?
10. Do you occasionally use information or skills from self-help books and workshops to manipulate others?
11. Do you usually think, "I don't care too much about what others think as long as I feel O.K. about what I do?"
12. Are you losing interest in your job, your old friends, and your general life style?

By talking to yourself about these kinds of questions you may learn whether or not excessive self-absorption is moving you toward a more conflict-prone life. If some unwarranted and useless conflict can possibly be avoided by this kind of internal dialog, why not give it a try?

Figure 3 illustrates another way of examining whether or not you are making yourself excessively vulnerable to conflict by focusing on social responsibility. Are you underresponsible (overly absorbed in yourself) or overresponsible (driven to please others and resenting it)?

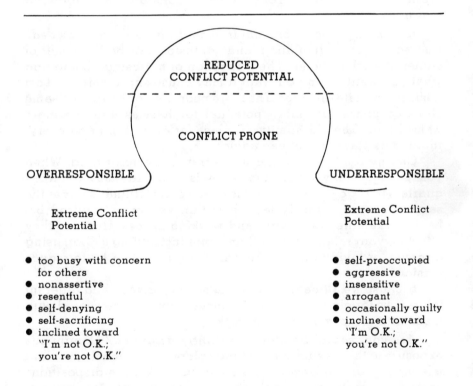

REDUCED
CONFLICT POTENTIAL

CONFLICT PRONE

OVERRESPONSIBLE

UNDERRESPONSIBLE

Extreme Conflict
Potential

Extreme Conflict
Potential

- too busy with concern for others
- nonassertive
- resentful
- self-denying
- self-sacrificing
- inclined toward "I'm not O.K.; you're not O.K."

- self-preoccupied
- aggressive
- insensitive
- arrogant
- occasionally guilty
- inclined toward "I'm O.K.; you're not O.K."

LOOK OUT FOR INCREASING COVERT OR PASSIVE-AGGRESSIVE CONFLICTS.

LOOK OUT FOR INCREASING CONFLICTS DUE TO OVERT AGGRESSION AND INSENSITIVITY.

Figure 3. Diagram of Overresponsible
and Underresponsible Traits

7. RECOGNIZE DAY-TO-DAY CONFLICT TRAPS

It isn't the mountain ahead that wears you out;
it's the grain of sand in your shoe.

One can easily become oblivious to conflict-producing factors in the everyday environment. As physical surroundings and human contacts become familiar, we tend to fall into routine behaviors and accept situations that can cause chronic problems. By consciously examining some easily overlooked facets of your environment you may identify something you wish to change in order to reduce avoidable conflict. Consider the following questions.

Is your home or work environment cluttered or crowded? Distraction, overstimulation, and confusion can be the result of clutter at work or home. The frustration of not being able to find what you want when you want it may cause short tempers. Lost items precipitate disputes. The more people who occupy the same cluttered space, the more potential for hassles and the more wasted time. The old homily "A place for everything and everything in its place" is not bad advice.

Closely related to clutter is the trap of overcrowding. When you put too many laboratory animals into extremely cramped quarters they go insane and attack each other. Humans under the same conditions quickly lose their thin veneer of civilized behavior. Examine your living and working spaces. How are they affecting your relationships? Sometimes just adding a door, using a screen, or laying down some carpeting may do a lot to reduce tensions.

Because we all have different needs for privacy and different tolerances for clutter, those differences should be discussed with those with whom you live and work.

Are your senses being unpleasantly assaulted? Continuous exposure to things such as clashing colors, continuously jangling telephones, or unpleasant odors can turn people's dispositions sour. As with clutter, offensive sensory overstimulation can precipitate all kinds of useless conflict so insidiously that one is scarcely aware of what is happening.

Step back and examine the places where you spend most of your time. Pinpoint the sources of your sensual aggravation, then do something about them. For example, modify the phone bell or experiment with life-supporting music. Instead of starting the day with the news or dissonant music, try Bach or Mozart. Use insulation and screens as well as stress-reducing colors. Hold meetings and conversations away from annoying noises such as the noisy hum of an air conditioner. Listen and watch for what works for you.

Do you find yourself in time binds—always rushing? Lack of planning and unrealistic perceptions of how much can be done in a given time can lead to disappointed children, enraged spouses, and aggravated co-workers. Nevertheless, time-related conflicts are among the most easily preventable, once you become aware of what is happening. How are you doing in this department? If the answer is "Not so well," consult Bliss (1976), Friedman and Rosenman (1978), and Lakein (1974).

Are you worried about your physical safety in your everyday environment? Working or living in a place that is perceived by you as unsafe can set your nerves on edge and keep them there even though you seem outwardly to "adjust." If you encounter a lot of heavy vehicular traffic, walk in high crime neighborhoods, or breathe polluted air, you are more likely to experience conflict with others. Do not "adjust" to such situations. Look into neighborhood-watch programs. Contact your local police for suggestions, and then make plans with supportive colleagues, friends, and neighbors for greater personal security. Taking any kind of action will partly relieve the anxiety and powerlessness that makes us more susceptible to defensive behavior and conflict.

Is your system of transportation adequate? Does your car run reliably? Can you depend on public transportation? Can you get where you want to go when you want to? Or are you missing appointments, being hassled by auto mechanics, or worrying about your dependency on others for transportation? Inadequate transportation can draw you into many useless conflicts. If this is happening, consider some alternatives. Make contingency plans for the time that your usual system of transportation may be disrupted. Keep a list of people who "go your way" or whom you can call in emergencies. Study alternative forms of transportation. An expansion of your options will reduce stress and conflict.

Do you perceive your personal finances realistically? Do you overspend, fail to anticipate needs, or otherwise live beyond your means? More family conflicts erupt over money than over any other single subject, regardless of income bracket. Money conflicts spill over into work environments, and personal debt is felt by some economists to be a leading cause of inflation. Take a realistic look at conflicts in your life that are precipitated by money. If you cannot solve them alone, professional help is available from consumer-affairs bureaus, banks, accountants, and credit and social-service agencies.

Are you oversubscribed and overcommitted to people? Many conflicts occur simply because a person is trying to juggle too many relationships and trying to meet the needs of too many people. Any relationship worth having requires energy to maintain. We have only a limited amount of energy. The question then becomes "How do we spend it?" or "Do we spend small amounts of energy on many superficial acquaintances or large amounts on a few significant and deep relationships?" Conflicts arise when we do not know what kind of human connections we want or when we try to maintain too many contacts with too little energy. Examine your own situation and see if it is the way you want it. If it is not, consider these two basic questions as guidelines:

a. Who are the significant others with whom I want most to be close? Write their names here:

b. How much energy do I put into maintaining these relationships? For example, in what kinds of things do I engage (meaningful conversations, phone calls, notes, thoughtful behavior, etc.)? Make a few notes below regarding changes you wish to make, insights, and ideas.

_____   _____

_____   _____

_____   _____

Are you well enough in tune with yourself to assess your physical and emotional condition continually? Unless you are feeling well, nothing much else seems to matter. Nevertheless, many people take better care of their cars than they do their bodies and then wonder why they are grumpy, out of sorts, quarrelsome, and always at odds with someone. Because our physical condition profoundly affects our emotions and our relationships with others, it may be useful to spend some time assessing your health. If you are interested in doing this, complete the following survey.

Personal Health Survey

Each of the items on the following inventory relates to some basic factor of well-being.

Directions: Answer as honestly as possible, writing out what first enters your mind as you read each question. When you have completed the survey, review the interpretation sheet.

   1. When was your last physical check up? How did it go?

   _____

   _____

   2. How would you assess your general health? What is your most common physical complaint (e.g., headache, tension, stomach ache, or skin problems)?

   _____

   _____

3. How does your energy level fluctuate throughout the day? What are your criteria or standards for measuring your energy?

_____

_____

4. What do you do for exercise? How often?

_____

_____

5. What recreation other than exercise do you participate in? How often?

_____

_____

6. Do you understand nutrition well enough to know when you are not eating "right"? What kinds of foods or beverages do not agree with you?

_____

_____

7. What person(s) do you feel comfortable confiding it?

_____

_____

8. What are your career or life goals?

_____

_____

9. How do you reward yourself for difficult accomplishments?

_____

10. What is important and valuable about your work?

_____

_____

Personal Health Survey
Interpretation Sheet

Review the following comments about the questions you just answered.

Questions 1, 2, and 3. Your answers should indicate your awareness of your physical well-being. A balance between over-concern about your health and a lack of sensitivity to your body signals is desirable.

Questions 4 and 5. Physical exercise is universally recommended as an important part of a vehicle for maintaining psycho-somatic equilibrium.

Question 6. Nutrition is a controversial topic, but one worth being aware of. At the very least, experiment to find out what foods work well in your body and how often and how much to eat to maintain optimal energy.

Question 7. Too much "holding in" of personal thoughts and feelings without confiding in anyone can reduce your personal and professional effectiveness and can even make you sick.

Question 8. Without at least some minimal goals, one tends to develop a certain loss of personal and/or professional power. This feeling of powerlessness is often translated into energy-robbing anxiety.

Question 9. This is a self-concept factor. If you don't think enough of yourself to reward yourself for doing well, who will? Self-affirmation is not the same as self-absorption.

Question 10. Most people's identities and feelings of self-worth are closely connected with their work or their jobs. If it is "just a job" and brings no joy or satisfaction, it may reduce your self-concept and also your life span.

List your insights about your degree of health and well-being and/or any changes you wish to make.

_____

_____

_____

_____

_____

_____

_____

_____

_____

Control over the basics of your personal environment is fundamental to effective conflict management. Cooperation with significant others on simple ways to deal with the above suggestions may help you view things differently as you renew your awareness of your overly familiar surroundings. More information about these and other personal-health categories may be found in books by Ardell (1977) and McCamy and Presley (1975).

8. AVOID ASSUMPTIONS

The human mind refuses to stay empty in spite of lack of information or understanding. When the mind is focused on something it knows nothing about, it fills in the blank spaces with assumptions. For example, when you talk on the telephone with people you have never seen, you probably make a mental picture of what they look like (an assumption). When going on vacation, you may assume that you will have a good time. These benign assumptions are not likely to cause any real trouble or conflict. However, when attempts are made to read minds or to stereotype people, beware! For a man today to assume that all women are content with previously expected roles is to invite conflict. To assume what another person's motivation might be in a touchy interpersonal relationship will only put us on the unproductive merry-go-round of "What I thought you meant was . . . " or "But I expected that you would . . . " or "If I had only known . . . " and so forth.

Why then do we continue to make assumptions? The answer is unknown and we will probably continue the practice indefinitely until it causes us more pain and aggravation than we want. At that point we can kick the assumption habit quite easily by doing two things. First, *check out the assumption.* Confront the individual as kindly and tactfully as possible. Ask about what is not clear to you. Listen very carefully to the response. Second, do not assume that you are being deceived. Each time that you have doubts about meaning, check it out again and again until you feel comfortable with what you are hearing. Because most human transactions are quite indirect we must resign ourselves to the necessity of politely and consistently validating information. By practicing this validation procedure you will find that it becomes less and less necessary as you become more skillful in listening and more accurate in your ability to understand others.

Also consider the other side of the coin and make it easy for others to avoid making assumptions about you. This is possible by being as clear as you can about your feelings and intentions. For example, when you are upset and grouchy, instead of making those around you miserable by pouting or saying, "There's nothing wrong; everything's just fine," let them know that you are out of sorts but that you will probably be all right in a while. Say something like "I'm really upset today" or "I'm mad as hell." If it is also true, you can add "But you're not the cause of it, and I'll be O.K. in a while." This simple procedure should help you avoid the destructive assumption game of "Guess why I'm feeling this way," a game that is sure to result in misunderstanding or worse.

Self-Check:

As you answer the following questions, think about how you are doing in avoiding and controlling assumptions.

- What do you usually do when you are not clear about an interpersonal message?
- What are your most persistent stereotypes? Think about categories such as racial-ethnic groups, elderly people, males, females, athletes, wealthy people, actors, etc.
- When was the last time you became involved in a conflict due to a misunderstanding? Were assumptions involved?
- How predictable are your feelings and intentions? Do you find that others have difficulty interpreting your behavior or are you easy to "read"?

If the answers to some of these questions are honestly "I don't know," you may be carrying a slight conflict-management handicap. Go back to Chapter 2 for some suggestions.

9. SENSITIVELY ANTICIPATE DESTRUCTIVE CONFLICT

Recognizing and positively confronting significant conflicts when they are small—thereby preventing them from escalating into unmanageable and destructive events—are valuable and learnable strategies. For this reason, this chapter will close with the description of a working model that you can use as part of your personal system of conflict management. The system goes a step beyond the avoidance of unwarranted conflict to the recognition, early confrontation, and possible prevention of important conflicts.

The Sherwood-Glidewell (1972) model for planned renegotiation is designed to help anticipate and prevent disruptive conflict before it destroys a significant relationship. It can be applied in any relationship that is intended to last for some period of time, whether it be as brief as part-time employment or as long lasting as a marriage contract. The model has four phases that describe the development of any human connection:[11]

---

[11]Adapted from: J.J. Sherwood and J.C. Glidewell. Planned Renegotiation: A Norm-Setting OD Intervention. In W.W. Burke (Ed.), *New Technologies in Organization Development: 1.* San Diego, CA: University Associates, 1972. Used with permission of John J. Sherwood.

Phase 1: Sharing information and negotiating expectations occur at the beginning of any relationship. Once an appropriate amount of negotiation and dialog takes place, uncertainty is reduced to an acceptable level. The forms of the negotiation and dialog depend on the situation. A short job interview would require a form much different from that of an extended courtship. The important point is that enough negotiation should take place for a future relationship to be apparent. Then commitment to the expectations can take place.

Phase 2: Commitment requires definitions of the roles so that each member knows, in general, what is expected of him or her, and each has a fairly clear picture of what to expect of the other(s). The more important the relationship, the more evidence of commitment required. For example, marriage implies a heavier commitment than living together, and a signed contract specifying certain behaviors and performance is more binding than a loose, verbal agreement.

Phase 3: Stability and productivity develop after roles have been established. People work together, friendships develop, and families are started. During this period the relationship stays acceptably predictable and comfortable for a period of time, but sooner or later a disruption will occur.

Phase 4: Disruption can occur for a variety of reasons: a new work location, unexpected job requirements, a new boss, a new child, an outside romantic interest in a spouse's life, a serious illness—anything that causes uncertainty, anxiety, or threat. When the disruption occurs, especially if there has not been adequate preparation and communication, strong forces come into play: (1) to return to the way things were, (2) to renegotiate, (3) to terminate the relationship, or (4) to live in pain. Unfortunately, returning to the way things were is rarely possible. Renegotiation is extremely difficult under the pressure of a major disruption,[12] and termination at this point is usually a resentful and unhappy process.

The reason for all this bad news is that when there is a disruption, anxiety and threat cause interpersonal communication and sensing systems to shut down just at the time when they most need to remain open so that adjustment and change can be facilitated.

---

[12]This is why marriage counseling has a rather poor success record and is now being referred to by many professionals as "marriage *and* divorce counseling."

The Planned Renegotiation Model (Figure 4) suggests that since disruptions are inevitable and destructive, they should be anticipated and all parties to the relationship should renegotiate expectations *in advance* of the "crunch" point. The model suggests that participants agree to renegotiate whenever anyone feels a "pinch" (a signal of an impending disruption). The one ground rule basic to this process is that any party to the relationship may call for renegotiation if a pinch is felt. The other parties must also participate in the renegotiation whether they feel a pinch or not. Some examples of pinches are the following:

- Lack of support: "You promised to work with me on that presentation and you never showed up."
- A surprise: "But it's 4:00 p.m. I can't possibly finish this by 4:30."
- Unusual behavior: "You've been acting funny lately; what's wrong?"
- Unilateral role redefinition: "Why are you going on a weekend skiing trip without me?"
- A rumor: "I heard that the next promotion is going to Jean. Is that true?"
- Loss of confidence in self or partner: "I'm not going to be able to keep these commitments unless I receive more help from you."
- Avoidance: "Although we're living in the same house, I feel that I have to make an appointment to talk with you. What's going on?"
- Doubts (not knowing the other's motivations): "I'd like to know why you're having to travel so much."
- Jealousy or envy: "Why can't I work on the new project with Bill? I've been here longer."
- Inability to predict: "I just don't know where I stand with you."
- Unexpected outside interference: "How long will your mother be staying?"
- Put-downs or criticism: "In front of your friends you talked to me as though I was retarded."
- Assumption: "I'm sure they won't mind—just this once."
- An intuitive reaction: "I don't know what it is, but I just don't feel right about our relationship."

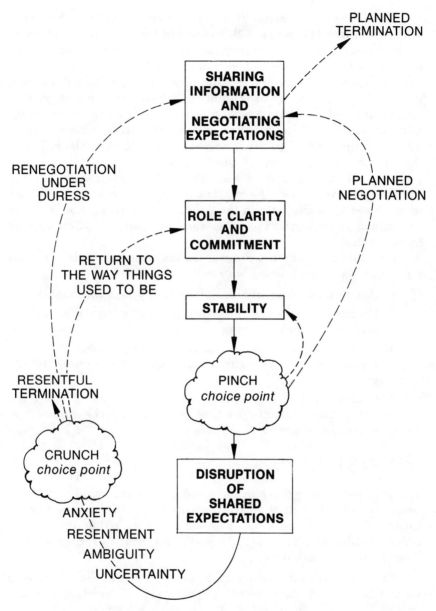

Figure 4. Planned Renegotiation Model

Reprinted from W.C. Boshear and K.G. Albrecht. *Understanding People: Models and Concepts.* San Diego, CA: University Associates, 1977. As adapted from Sherwood and Glidewell (1972). Used with permission of John J. Sherwood.

The keys to preventing destructive conflict through the use of this model are (1) desire, (2) understanding, (3) recognition of mutual payoff, and (4) commitment to the process. First, parties must *want* to invest some energy in maintaining the relationship. Second, they must understand the process, especially the subtle notion that an anxiety-producing pinch—although felt by one individual—when shared will make others in the relationship anxious and that this is a risk that must willingly be shared if problem solving and productive change are to take place. Third, they must recognize that if planned renegotiation takes place, payoff to all parties in the relationship will be far greater than the limited options following a major disruption. Finally, all parties must agree to participate in the process, and *all* parties must be committed to renegotiating roles and expectations when *anyone* feels pinched.

If you decide that this process makes sense and has value for you, consider the following way to use it:

1. Read this section with the other(s) in your relationship.
2. Discuss the process until you are satisfied that all involved understand how it works.
3. Keep a diagram of the Planned Renegotiation Model in plain sight as a reminder of your commitment to the process.
4. Check with the other(s) from time to time to keep the commitment strong so that pinches will be allowed to surface and not be suppressed.

COMMENT

The nine sections in this chapter suggest ways to avoid or prevent dead-end or unproductive conflicts in order to save energy for those all-too-frequent times when conflict is either completely unavoidable or is necessary to solve important problems. Look them over one more time.

Section 1 asks if you are clear enough about the issues and values in your life to differentiate between the kinds of conflict that make a difference and the kinds that are best avoided.

Section 2 provides questions to help you determine whether or not your expectations of others are realistic.

Section 3 asks if your relationships with significant others are balanced well enough to prevent feeling guilty because you owe someone or resentful because you are owed. Guilt and resentment are prime contributors to destructive conflict.

Section 4 suggests that you avoid *all* negative criticism of others (or at least explore alternative behaviors as substitutes for criticism) and that you examine ways to reduce conflict caused by criticism directed at you.

Section 5 suggests reducing the conflict in your life by forcing yourself to actively cultivate optimistic attitudes and behaviors in the face of problems and conflicts.

Section 6 asks if you have become so self-aware and self-preoccupied that the conflicts in your life are increasing because of a lack of sensitivity and responsibility to others. It asks if your life is comfortably balanced between realistic self-awareness and appropriate social responsibility.

Section 7 suggests becoming more aware of the numerous, everyday, conflict-causing factors.

Section 8 suggests that much interpersonal conflict can be avoided by checking out all assumptions before acting on them.

Section 9 presents a model for dealing with conflicts before they become serious enough to destroy a relationship.

Chapter 4

How To Handle Unavoidable Conflict

I thought I saw a light at the end of the tunnel, but it turned out to be a freight train coming from the other direction.

Unknown

Regardless of what we do to keep conflicts at a tolerable minimum, we inevitably are faced with a number of interpersonal disruptions. They can range from routine disagreements to acts of physical violence. How successfully such events are handled depends on a person's skill in selecting the behaviors that most appropriately match his or her style *and* the situation.

This chapter describes some ideas and strategies that can help you make more positive and effective choices when that unavoidable conflict enters your life. It begins with several techniques for developing greater self-control and then deals with the basic conflict-related emotion, *anger*, and suggests ways to handle it. A number of specific communication concepts emphasize sending and receiving strategies that were specifically selected for their usefulness in managing conflict. A discussion of the advantages and disadvantages of using humor is followed by twenty ideas for handling yourself in previolent conflict situations.

HOW TO STRENGTHEN CONTROL OVER YOURSELF

Handling conflict requires—more than anything else—the self-discipline of controlling the emotions that conflict produces. When faced with an unpleasant interpersonal situation, a person generally deals with it in old ways that have often not worked well. If you are among that small and fortunate minority that handles conflicts without discomfort, then read no farther. Otherwise, the following suggestions may help.

66

Systematic Desensitization. When you know a conflict is inevitable and you have some lead time, the following techniques may help reduce the impact and enable you to develop greater control of yourself. The more time you have before the conflict, the greater the desensitization effect.

1. Sit comfortably in a chair. Close your eyes and relax. Follow the relaxation procedures described in Chapter 7.

2. Imagine the impending conflict in vivid detail and living color. Make pictures in your head of the physical location, the opening remarks, the clothes being worn, the temperature of the room, and every detail you can conjure up.

3. Play the scene in your mind until you find yourself becoming tense. (Tightness around the mouth and in the neck and arms is usually a good indicator.) This may happen almost immediately. When it does, say to yourself, "Stop." Open your eyes. Do something pleasant or distracting.

4. When you begin to feel less tense, go back to your relaxed state through deep breathing, counting, or whatever works for you.

5. When you are feeling serene again, take up where you left off in picturing the conflict situation.

6. Continue this procedure until you actually face the conflict. This method gives your body the necessary training to relax under the pressure of an anticipated situation.

This type of behavioral rehearsal is often practiced by successful athletes who want to gain control over their anxieties before a pressure event.

"Psyching Down" Through Relaxation. A New York City police officer who specializes in hostage release and other high risk confrontations recently stated in a national television interview that when approaching a volatile and physically dangerous case, he works hard at getting himself "down" for the confrontation. For example, he listens to soothing music in the police car instead of activating the siren. If it seems practical, he will slow down his driving speed or do anything he can to relax physically.

Conditioning ourselves to relax will make us more effective under the pressure of conflict. Relaxation reduces the dissonance in our brains and enables us to think more clearly. Edmund Jacobsen, the originator of progressive-relaxation techniques, suggests procedures for training yourself to relax on cue. By alternately contracting and relaxing specific muscles, you can learn to recognize when situations are making you tense. Once you have mastered deep-relaxation techniques, momentary or instantaneous relaxation under duress becomes easier. Detailed information and step-by-step relaxation procedures can be found in books by Benson and Klipper (1975), Jacobsen (1978), and Walker (1975).

Centering and Self-Monitoring. When conflict strikes and your ego is threatened, stop for a moment and scan yourself. Slow down the dialog and take a moment to get a clear sense of your own boundaries. Ask yourself:

- Am I clearly in touch with what is going on inside of me, i.e., my *real* emotions, instead of what I would like them to be?
- Am I focused on what is going on *right here and now* rather than what might happen or what has happened?
- Am I physically centered at this moment? Does my body language indicate that I am in control of myself?

By checking yourself with such questions whenever you are involved in any kind of interpersonal transaction you will develop a growing sense of where you end and where others begin. This sense of self is invaluable in building the confidence necessary for handling conflict. You can practice every day; do not wait for a disruptive event.

Putting it in Perspective. Believing "This, too, shall pass" can be extremely liberating in difficult confrontations. The wisdom that comes by living through many conflicts teaches that most situations rarely turn out as badly as we imagine.

A realistic and balanced perspective can be developed by asking questions such as "How important would this conflict be if:"

- I were looking back on it a year from now?
- I knew that I had but six months to live?
- I were informed that my spouse, child, or other loved one had been seriously injured?
- I knew we were about to undergo a nuclear attack?

Another great leveler can be a temporary illness. It is remarkable how those critically important matters do not seem so important when you are vomiting into a porcelain fixture. Your perspective has changed.

Although a serious conflict should not be treated casually or capriciously, the situation should be mentally monitored realistically enough to be kept in its proper place as it relates to one's total life.

Examining Ogres. The question to ask when feeling overwhelmed by a conflict with a seemingly formidable adversary or set of circumstances is "What is the worst thing that could happen?" The answer will help calibrate the threat and explore the options. When we examine all the ogres that we have created in our minds and take realistic looks at our catastrophic expectations, they rarely seem as frightening as originally imagined. This kind of internal dialog is an effective antidote to the infinite capacity of the human mind for self-intimidation. Becoming aware that our ogres originate in our brains and can be controlled at the source will stop us from discounting ourselves and giving our power away to others. Can you think of the last time you created a conflict ogre for yourself? They often visit in the night and scare the devil out of you. Next time this happens before, during, or after the conflict, remember to ask the question, "What's the worst thing that could happen?"—and watch your ogre shrink.

Thought Stopping or Diversion. In the middle of an intense conflict we may feel all kinds of anxiety-producing thoughts entering our minds. By consciously and rationally blocking these thoughts, our emotional equilibrium can be restored. Thought stopping is a technique that can easily be learned. When an unwanted or disturbing thought enters your mind, imagine that you are hearing the word STOP shouted loudly in your ear. This causes your brain temporarily to come to a halt and enables you to regain your composure.

Practice the technique of thought stopping or diversion (switching to more pleasant or productive thoughts) during quiet times when you are not engaged in conflict. If no one is around, you can shout "stop" out loud when destructive thoughts visit you. Some behaviorists suggest placing a rubber band on the wrist and snapping it vigorously enough to cause pain when unwanted thoughts appear. Continuous practice in eliminating negative self-talk will increase one's ability to transcend the stress of conflict.

Countless other systems for developing greater control of one's self are available to a serious student who is willing to spend the necessary time. Yoga, meditation in many forms, biofeedback, autogenics, and various kinds of hypnosis offer endless possibilities (see Lande, 1976; LeShan, 1974; A. Smith, 1975; Werthman, 1978).

HOW TO HANDLE ANGER

When facing an unavoidable interpersonal conflict, chances are great that you are dealing with overt or disguised anger—your own or someone else's. I cannot imagine a conflict in which anger or its companion emotion, fear, are not heavy contributors. What to do in the face of these emotions may require some new ways of thinking and behaving. The following three steps may help.

1. Understand how anger develops. Ask a few people what makes them angry. They will probably point to some source outside of themselves, such as a supervisor, pushy people, or rude children. They rarely mention threat or fear as a cause of their anger. The lack of personal awareness regarding such a powerful emotion is one reason why many small conflicts escalate out of proportion.

Jones and Banet (1976) describe anger in the following way:[13]

> Although anger seems to be a response to something outside of us, it most often is an *intra*personal event: we make ourselves angry. But because anger is so unpleasant and human beings are so adept at projection, we usually attempt to locate the source of our anger outside ourselves with statements such as "You make me angry," "You have irritating habits," "You bother me."
>
> When we perceive an external event as threatening to our physical or psychological well-being, a cycle of internal movements is initiated. As the perception is formed, assumptions are made internally about the possible danger of the threat. The assumption is then checked against our perceived power of dealing with the threat. If we conclude that the threat is not very great or that we are powerful enough to confront it successfully, a calm, unflustered response can occur. But if we conclude that the threat is dangerous or that we are powerless to handle it, anger emerges in an effort to destroy or reduce the personal threat and to protect our assumed impotency. The anger cycle can be graphically represented [see Figure 5]. (p. 111)

An intellectual understanding of anger, however, is not enough. The next step relates to what to do about it.

2. Learn to deal positively with your anger. Any unlabeled feeling is a potential source of conflict and pain, but unidentified

---

[13]Reprinted from: J.E. Jones and A.G. Banet, Jr. Dealing with Anger. In J.W. Pfeiffer and J.E. Jones (Eds.), *The 1976 annual handbook for group facilitators.* San Diego, CA: University Associates, 1976. Used with permission.

anger can be particularly destructive, because it can disguise itself in many ways. Lack of a clear sense of our reaction to anger is a serious handicap in dealing with the emotional fallout of conflict. We need to know not only *what* pushes our anger button, but also how we generally *behave* when it is pushed, i.e., with denial, withdrawal, displacement, depression, violence, etc. Self-understanding is essential to ridding ourselves of behaviors that are not working well.

When you first realize that your anger is rising, several procedures, also based on the work of Jones and Banet, may help. The first and perhaps most important thing to do is to acknowledge your anger. *Own it and admit that it belongs only to you.* For example, the co-worker who arranged for you to be stuck with the bulk of the work for which both of you were responsible did not *make* you angry. Nor did the person who stole your parking spot. They were just taking care of their needs at your expense. You alone generated the anger, so claim it. By so doing you will increase your sense of personal power. According to Jones and Banet (1976, p. 112), "It increases self-awareness and prevents unwarranted blaming of others. Turning blame and attribution into I statements locates the anger where it actually is—inside us."

Next, calibrate your response by asking yourself, "Just how angry am I?" Your anger will probably range from mild to

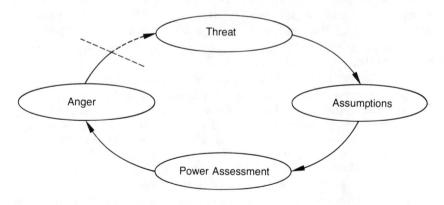

Figure 5. The Anger Cycle

See footnote 13.

intense. By assessing the level of your anger you will be able to make better judgments regarding what to do about it. This may help avoid inappropriate action that would only escalate a conflict.

Diagnose the threat. Remember the anger cycle? If you are not frightened, you probably will not become angry; so ask yourself, "What is frightening about the perceived threat? What do I stand to lose?" Back off and examine the threat. It may not be as bad as you think.

Next, talk to people about the perceived threat. This method will help you better understand what is bothering you. The feedback you receive will probably clear up your perceptions of the situation and defuse your anger. It may even turn the situation into something to laugh at.

Finally, accept forgiveness as the terminal way of letting go of anger. In the words of Jones and Banet (1976, p. 112), "Forgiving and forgetting cleans the slate and is a way of opening yourself to future transactions. Forgiveness is a magnanimous gesture that increases personal power." Admittedly, this is easy to say and difficult to do, mainly because many people in organizations perceive forgiveness as a sign of weakness. The prevailing attitude seems to be "A true professional never gets mad—just gets even." Nevertheless, forgiveness does have practical value. First, forgiveness enables you to stop looking over your shoulder and wondering what your antagonist is going to do next. Second, you can stop draining off your energy figuring out either how to avoid contact or how to get even. Third, re-establishing a positive relationship with someone who was formerly an antagonist will strengthen your confidence in your ability to confront and deal with conflict.

Van Nuys (1975) has some additional thoughts:[14]

> When your guts are churning, your breathing is short, your voice is getting clipped, or loud, or unusually soft; or you're getting obliquely sarcastic, but doing your damndest to suppress it; that is not detachment. That's denial. And I don't think denial is healthy, intraphysically or interpersonally. Whether or not you need to scream or pound pillows at that point, I don't know. But I do think it is important to own your anger and deal with it in some way.

> I don't believe we need to react to every little slight with an outburst of anger to keep our insides clean. I believe we can and must learn to

---

[14]Reprinted from: D. Van Nuys. Dealing with Anger: Detachment or Denial. Copyright © 1975. *Human Behavior* Magazine. Reprinted by permission.

know what's going on in our insides. I believe we can evolve personally, if not collectively, toward a broader awareness in which more and more we can truly say "It ain't no big thing" and just let it slip by. I think that must be what the mystics mean by detachment— letting go of it, completely. But evolution is slow, and if you or I rush into clerical robes too fast, pretending to let go while secretly holding on—that's denial. (p. 15)

3. Learn to confront anger in others effectively. Overheated interpersonal conflicts in which anger is the dominant emotion represent the times when we most often need to apply the most effective human relations skills, yet they also represent the times when we are cerebrally short-circuiting. Selective practice of the following suggestions may help in dealing with anger in others.

- Do not get hooked by anger. Anger expressed by others can draw us into conflicts that are none of our business. During meetings, for example, employees who are hooked by their own reactions to particular personalities easily become involved in conflicts when they may not even disagree with the basic issues. A threat presented by a particular person is unconsciously converted into anger, which—in turn—pulls the entire meeting off track. As soon as you discover that you are being drawn into this type of situation, ask yourself, "Whose problem is this? What do I have to gain by becoming involved?" Then listen carefully to your answers.

- Temporarily abandon the need to be logical. It is futile to try to dissolve fear or anger in others through logic. Emotions simply are not responsive to reason. In fact, reason is likely to intensify an emotion. When you apply reason, you make others feel irrational in expressing their emotions and thereby block them from doing so. This blocking increases tension instead of resolving conflict. If you have ever tried to talk someone out of a fear of the dark, of water, of airplanes, of dogs, or of anything else, you must have experienced the uselessness of logic in dealing with emotions. Still it is difficult to resist trying, because faith in the power of logic to control human reactions dies hard. Think about an employee who has given blood, sweat, tears, and overtime to a project. You are the one who must turn it down because of unanticipated budget cuts. The employee, properly or not, blows sky high. This is definitely not the time for logical persuasion. You really have no effective choice but to listen and deal with the disappointment and anger. The next time you encounter an emotional reaction in someone and find yourself reaching for a piece of logic to dispel his emotion, give it up. It will not work and it might only worsen the situation. Instead, acknowledge the anger coming your way by saying something like "You really seem furious" or "I can see how you feel." Any *appropriate* statement that fits your style and the importance of the emotion will often cool down the situation.

- State how *you* feel and what *you* want as clearly and as pleasantly as possible. Be sure to indicate the intensity of your own feelings so that the possibilities of being misunderstood are reduced.

- Be reasonable but stick to your principles and your bottom lines (see Chapter 3). Manuel J. Smith (1975) calls this type of persistent reasonableness "broken record." It is the skill of calm repetition—saying what you want over and over without becoming hostile or loud until you are finally heard.

- Train yourself to renege on statements made in the heat of anger. As difficult as it may be to "give in," the payoff can be considerable. A statement such as "I was angry and upset when I said that" can often clear the air and lower the tension. In a stand-off someone has to make the first conciliatory gesture, and it might as well be you. Hanging tough and holding the line usually only prolongs the hostilities.

- Ignore abuse; only respond—verbally or nonverbally—to reasonable statements. This technique will tend to extinguish unfair and off-the-wall verbiage. It requires no defensiveness on your part, although you may have to practice desensitizing yourself to angry outbursts (see Chapter 4).

- Avoid escalation: Try negotiating an agreement with the other person(s) to lower the voice level and control verbal abuse so that discussion can continue. If this does not work after a reasonable time, then abandon the interaction.

Confronting anger is not easy, because many people regard anger as "not nice" and as an emotion to be avoided at all costs. It is no wonder that we become confused and react inappropriately in the face of this powerful emotion, so before you decide to practice anger-confrontation skills, study these suggestions.

a. Start slowly, first in the role of an observer. Look for situations in which anger and threat are involved and watch what happens. Notice how antagonists deal with one another. Make mental notes about how you might handle it differently. Ask yourself, "What would I do or say in this situation?" As you read the above text, reflect on your style and your options, keeping in mind behaviors that "fit" for you.

b. Think about what provokes anger in you. What threatens you the most? What kinds of people? What kinds of situations? What merely annoys you and what enrages you? Make a list of these things and assign an intensity value from 1 to 10 (1 for lowest and 10 for highest) to each item.

_____   _____

_____   _____

_____   _____

_____   _____

_____   _____

c. Imagine some situations that might provoke anger in you. Check your list and work through a few of them using the systematic desensitization process described at the beginning of this chapter.

d. Gradually involve yourself in situations in which anger is likely to develop and try out your self-control strategies. Move from low threat encounters to more difficult ones. It is up to you to decide how to go with this. Just remember that this process is much like the physical conditioning of an athlete. It takes work.

As your confidence increases through the development and practice of anger-confrontation skills, you will begin to take more and more risks. When starting out, however, it is difficult to predict how your behavior will be perceived. Therefore, if you have tried everything you know and if the high anger situation is still escalating (i.e., verbal abuse, threats, and potential for violence), protect yourself by leaving the scene with as much grace as possible. To persist under such conditions can be exhausting, fruitless, and dangerous. The defusion of potentially violent conflicts in discussed later in this chapter.

FOURTEEN STRATEGIES FOR CONFLICT COMMUNICATION

Communicating under conditions of interpersonal conflict calls for an orientation different from that of everday conversation. The possibilities for misunderstanding and painful disruption of relationships in conflict situations require the use of specialized strategies, a number of which are described on the following pages.

Although these ideas have been used widely with generally positive results, it is important for you to examine them in terms of how they fit *your personal style* before trying them out.

1. Put your tendency to judge on hold. When emotions are at fever pitch, it is difficult to resist the natural inclination to make judgments. However, that is exactly what we must do, even if it means choking on our good intentions. Nothing escalates a conflict faster than a judgmental comment. A basic fact of life is that when we feel that we are being judged and our values and competence are being questioned, we become anxious, resistant, and sometimes hostile.

If during a confrontation you feel the need to make a judgmental comment, bite your tongue and make a *descriptive* one instead. For example:

"You cut me off in midsentence" instead of

"You have this aggravating habit of interrupting."

or

"You agreed to set up the meeting and it never happened," followed by a questioning silence, instead of

"It was irresponsible of you not to keep your agreeement to set up the meeting. How can I count on you?"

Describe only what you see or what has happened without implying blame or interpreting motives. Try to do it with as pleasant an expression as you can muster under the circumstances and let the other person take it from there. It will be much easier to move out of conflict and into problem solving if you do not have to deal with the resistance triggered by judging. Also see the comments on criticism in Chapter 3.

2. *Deal with present behavior.* In managing our lives it is usually not very helpful to deal with the dead past or to make assumptions about an uncertain future. The resurrection of past injustices or the prediction of future catastrophes is especially nonproductive in conflict situations. Movement away from the present situation tends to block the real issues.

> Suggestion: Whenever you realize that the dialog is probing into the past or future (except for necessary and appropriate information), use one of these questions: "How can that help us here?" or "What can we do about what's going on right now?"

3. *Pay attention to the music.* The music of communication consists of the nonverbal behaviors that accompany the words. It is postulated that 50 to 80 percent of the meaning within a human transaction is communicated by body language and voice inflection. It is these behaviors that often give us trouble in conflict situations as we try to camouflage our emotions with words. If words and music are not congruent, we run the risk of mixed messages, confusion, and escalation.

An effective way to locate your optimum level of nonverbal behavior is to study the following continuums. Read each of the four categories in Figure 6 and estimate how your behavior might be perceived by a person whom you would be confronting. Place a mark on the line where you see yourself. Then check out your perception with someone who knows you well. If you are not satisfied, try out some new nonverbal behaviors next time you interact with someone. Practice in a low threat, nonconflict encounter until you feel comfortable with your new behavior. It does not take a monumental change to produce results. Sometimes an almost imperceptible pause or a slight shift of body position or facial expression will convey an entirely different feeling tone.

Voice qualities such as loudness, rate of speech, fluency, and intonation are additional factors that can soothe or aggravate. How are you doing in all of these categories?

Both physical and behavioral scientists are making specific observations that have interesting implications for human communication. For example, Leonard (1978) discusses in some detail the fundamental rhythm of verbal and nonverbal communication between speakers and listeners. He asserts, "At the most fundamental level, the listener is not reacting or responding

Eye Contact

Avoidance; shifty
eye movements

Hard and unblinking
stare

(Practice focusing on various parts of a person's face until you become comfortable with direct eye contact. From four feet away, people cannot tell where you are looking.)

Facial Expression

Misfit with
verbal message

Perfect fit
with verbal message

(Some people smile when they are angry, talk about happiness with a pained look on their faces, or have no expression at all. If you are to be taken seriously, there must be some consistency between your face and your words.)

Gestures

Hardly any
movement

Extreme
animation

(Movement of the body must also match the verbal message. Inappropriate gestures can confuse and distract. When in doubt, be economical with your movements. Be aware also of excessive coughing, blinking, and other mannerisms that may cause confusion or misinterpretation of the message.)

Body Orientation

Slumped and
leaning-away stance

Direct, face-to-face,
head-on stance

(A modified frontal stance angled about 20 degrees from face-to-face posture seems to be most acceptable for confrontation that reflects assertiveness but not belligerence or passivity.)

**Figure 6. Continuua for Self-Ranking
Nonverbal Behaviors**

to the speaker. The listener is in a sense *part of, one with* the speaker" (p. 18).

The speaker and listener, according to Leonard, are measurably synchronized. This may be an explanation for the popular and elusive term "vibes" that is so often used and abused in describing human interaction.

4. Use "I" messages. The "I" message is designed to help communicate feelings congruently and to deal with the problem behavior in a manner that will produce voluntary change while maintaining the quality of the relationship. The ideal "I" message includes the following three elements in any order.

- A description of problem *behavior* stated in a way that gives the other person a clear idea about what was done without arousing excessive defensiveness. The description must be specific, and blame-loaded words or intonations must be avoided.
- Feelings evoked in you by the behavior. This is the "I" part of the message, and it allows the other person to experience the intensity of your concern.
- A description of the tangible effects on you. If the other person can see the effect of the behavior, change is more likely. This part of the message helps you avoid criticism and moralizing.

Examples:

a. When you come to work at 9:00 and leave at 3:00 (description) I really worry (feeling), because I have three annual reports that must be done on time (effect).

b. When your clothes are all over the floor (description) I feel frustrated and angry (feeling), because I don't have time to do all my work and pick up your clothes, too (effect).

With practice, the formula "BEHAVIOR + FEELINGS + EFFECT" (in any order) will become easier and easier to use. Try it out in any situation in which you are angry and at a loss for what to say or when you feel that whatever you say will sound accusatory and probably be misunderstood. Some typical situations might be the following:

- Because an employee is constantly late to staff meetings, you always have to repeat important information;
- Someone chronically fails to return your phone calls;
- Your assistant fails to keep you informed, and you have repeatedly been embarrassed because you did not have all of the facts; and
- You are disappointed in the low quality performance of a usually dependable person.

Practice in these types of situations, or try the formula out at home when you are aggravated by a member of the family. You can also use it when shopping or conducting low threat transactions with clerks, parking attendants, waiters, etc.

5. Apply strategic openness. It is easy to be seduced by the many prevalent "pop-psych" approaches to managing conflict that advocate "letting it all hang out," "telling it like it is," or being totally "up front." Although such honesty and forthrightness is commendable, it is not always an optimal strategy in conflict situations. In fact, inappropriate openness often interferes with communication and may produce unexpected and even disastrous results. The concept of *strategic openness*[15] is a helpful way of finding balance between complete candor and the unproductive silence accompanying withdrawal and denial.

The powerful defenses we erect to protect the way we see ourselves become even stronger when these self-perceptions are threatened. With this concept in mind it may be more productive to be strategically open rather than calling it exactly the way we see it. For example, a sales manager might be faced with a situation that goes something like this:

> Joe thinks of himself as an outstanding salesman. On the basis of what he has delivered, however, he is nothing special. I tell him so in his monthly evaluation conference. I point out his weak new-accounts record, his declining performances, and what I perceive as some minor abuses of his draw and his expense account. I lay it right on the line and confront Joe with total openness.

They now have a serious conflict of perceptions. Joe thinks he is doing an outstanding job. The manager tells him he is on the low side of average. This situation has all the ingredients for an escalation of conflict, either openly or covertly. This kind of scenario is probably played out thousands of times each day in homes and offices. Strategic openness can reduce or defuse the conflict potential of such confrontations if we can learn to avoid deception yet prevent the encounter from being blown apart by insensitivity. To do this it is essential to *work at understanding how others see themselves.*

The following points may help you decide how much of yourself to share verbally with another person when you are in situations with high conflict potential.

- Openness is justifiable only when readiness and willingness for honest interchange have been established. This takes time and is more profitably done *before* a conflict develops (see the sensitive-anticipation model in Chapter 3).
- Strategic openness means being just a bit more open with your thoughts and feelings than you think the people in the

---

[15]For more on strategic openness, see Pfeiffer and Jones (1972).

system can stand. The motive is to encourage some recipro-
cal honesty, thereby leading to more effective communication. Your openness, however, should never be threatening enough to cause others to close up.

● In our preoccupation with honesty we may miss the point
so well made by Powell (1974, p. 137), "The genius of
communication is the ability to be both totally honest and
totally kind at the same time."

● Openness requires trust and should be based on intent to
help or solve problems rather than to manipulate. It is
sometimes helpful to negotiate openness by asking, "What
is O.K. to talk about in this situation and what is not O.K.?"

● Finally, openness—contrary to popular misinformation—is
not a panacea for communication, problem solving, or
conflict management. It is not intelligent or productive, for
example, to be open with someone who will use your
revelations to hurt you.

Experiment with strategic openness in relatively low threat
situations with people who are not highly significant in your life
before practicing at home or at work.

In summary, the recommended process of strategic openness
involves testing what you say against these questions:

   a. Can the other person handle what I am telling him or her
   without becoming defensive?

   b. Do I *need* to tell everything that I am planning to tell in
   order to get my message across? Am I telling more than I
   should tell?

   c. Will my message improve or aggravate the situation?

   6. Choose your words carefully. The words used in a confrontation can profoundly affect the outcome. For example,
quoting school rules and regulations to irate parents whose child
has just been suspended will aggravate the problem, as will any
excess use of bureaucratic jargon.

Certain words will guarantee escalation. "Don't," "ought,"
"should," "always," "never" and "must" tend to sound like words
that a stern and critical parent would use when scolding a small,
helpless child. Quite naturally, defensiveness, anger, and even
hostility are often provoked whenever the "child" part of us is
hooked by someone else's "critical-parent" words.[16]

---

[16]For more information about child, parent, and adult ego states and
other transactional-analysis terms, see James and Jongeward (1975).

In sending messages, it is difficult enough to penetrate the prejudicial filters of others without the added handicap of a red-flag vocabulary. Think about the words that trigger your hostility and tone them down by learning to euphemize strategically. By substituting soft words for hard words you can improve conflict communication. For example, instead of calling something an "issue," which is almost guaranteed to force people to take sides, try using the term "situation that needs attention." Substitute "sanction" for "punishment," "heated discussion" for "argument," and so on. This strategy does not require unrealistic or non-assertive behavior, but just enough care to prevent communication from being unnecessarily terminated because of an inappropriate choice of words.

   7. Give permission to withhold information. Conflicts are sometimes difficult to manage due to the reluctance of some people to be honest about their true feelings. A technique for getting reluctant people to open up to you is to give them permission to withhold information. Say something like "Just tell me whatever you feel comfortable with. If there's anything you don't want to say, that's perfectly O.K." Giving people permission to withhold usually increases the likelihood that they will tell you more.

   These first seven items have focused on the *sending* strategies. The real payoff in conflict communication, however, is in the proper use of *receiving* strategies. This means *listening effectively,* something that is difficult when things are going well and that becomes painfully difficult when we are faced with conflict and opposition.

   Volumes have been written about the complexities of listening. If one were to study all the reasons why effective listening is so difficult, the path of least resistance would be to stop listening entirely. Instead, the process can be simplified by breaking listening into two components: *attending* and *responding.* Attending simply means "*being with,*" that is, paying attention with all your senses to the person with whom you are attempting to communicate. It also means demonstrating interest and encouragement by using appropriate verbal and nonverbal signals. Attending requires considerable energy, but the payoff is great. By completely "being with" someone with whom we are in a conflict dialog, our chances of more effectively managing the conflict will be infinitely greater. On the other hand, if we fail to use our sensing equipment appropriately because of inattention, any conflict in which we are participating can easily get out of control.

The following four-step check list has been used by participants in many workshops and seminars as a memory aid to be kept in the forefront of their consciousness when conflict communication begins. It is helpful in improving one's ability to attend.

When I am in a confrontation with another person, how well do I:

1. *Encourage?*

   Do I demonstrate interest and attentiveness by using encouraging nonverbal behavior, i.e., friendly eye contact, posture, attentive head nodding, etc.?

2. *Stay quiet?*

   Do I allow enough silence? Do I listen more than talk?

3. *Hold back criticism?*

   Do I curb my natural impulse to criticize until my antagonist has "poured it all out," and then do I respond in a nonargumentative way?

4. *Listen actively?*

   Do I pick up on the verbal and nonverbal clues that help me listen "between the lines" and pay attention to the emotions involved?

If you will work on at least one of these four steps of attending the next time you are under the pressure of conflict communication, a few barriers should come down and you will stand a better chance of selecting a more effective response style.

After exercising your skill in attending, you have a wide choice of response options. Items 8 through 14 include seven do-and-don't suggestions. Experiment with them and use what works for you.

8. Restate or paraphrase what you hear. This technique involves repeating for clarification what was said by another person. It is useful when long, complicated sentences or confusing speech patterns obscure the essential message. Restatement is also helpful in cutting the jargon that often develops in tense situations as antagonists attempt to prove to one another how much they know. The repetition of another's idea in clear, simple language is also a way of checking for meaning during telephone conversations when nonverbal clues are not available.

Whenever another's statement is paraphrased, it needs to be followed by a "check out" question such as "Did I understand you correctly?" or "Is that your message?"

Caution: If overused, restatement can be perceived as a put down, especially if you try to oversimplify a long and complicated statement into a short sentence. Paraphrasing can also turn into "parroting" and cause counterproductive irritation. Also avoid cliches, such as "What I hear you saying is . . ."

9. *Use reflection or active-listening strategies.* Reflection involves a two-step process of (1) listening so carefully to the statements of others that one can fully understand their meaning and perceive the feelings behind the words and (2) periodically verifying one's perceptions by reflecting the feelings underlying the speaker's statements. The following are examples of reflective remarks:

- Your supervisor did not listen to your explanation, and you are really ticked off.
- You seem upset by some of the things I've done lately.
- It sounds as though your boss is causing you a lot of frustration.

People need to know that their feelings, as well as their statements, are being understood. Skillful use of active listening can often calm down volatile situations.

Caution: Do not rush the process; beginning active listeners may distort messages by exaggeration or interpretation, may slip into advice giving in order to save time, or may use irritating pseudopsychological cliches.

10. *Beware of questions.* Although questions sometimes assist conflict resolution, more often they tend to aggravate the communication. Often questions are used as an attack. Disguised statements or pseudoquestions confuse meanings and punish the recipient. Here are a few examples:

- The co-optative or "gotcha" question (an attempt to manipulate in order to obtain the response one wants or to "set up" another person):
  Don't you think that . . . ?
  Isn't it true that . . . ?
  Do you still . . . ?
  Weren't you the one who . . . ?
- The punitive question (an attempt to put another person on the spot or to make an unprepared or weaker person look foolish):
  Why did you make that decision?
  Where did you get your information?

- Imperative question (an implied command):
  When will you be ready?
  Have you done it yet?
- Screened question (an attempt to avoid a direct statement):
  Would you like Chinese food?
  Do you love me?
- Rhetorical question (an attempt to obtain agreement):
  That was a dumb statement, right?
  She really isn't qualified, you know?
  We'll work on this together, O.K.?

If you are a victim of pseudoquestioning, use the following phrases to put the communication back on a productive track.

- That sounds like a statement, and I could deal with it better in that way. Let me rephrase it.
- Tell me what you are saying. That doesn't sound like a real question.
- What are you *telling* me with that question?
- Do you really want that question answered?

Inappropriate questioning blocks authentic communication, because the true motivation of the questioner is often hidden. It would be a mistake, however, to view all questions as bad. It depends on whether or not the question is useful in dealing with the conflict. Questions can be legitimately used to do the following:

- Obtain information,
- Reduce anxiety and tension,
- Deflect touchy subjects,
- Fulfill recognition needs, and
- Draw out responses.

Why, what, and how questions require special attention. A good general rule is to avoid asking "why" questions whenever possible, because they are often answered in vague ways that contribute little to problem solving. "Why" questions are also perceived as probes and therefore engender resistance and unhelpful answers. Here are a few examples of the answers that "why" questions can foster:

- "Why won't you go with me?" "Because I don't feel like it."
- "Why did you do that?" "I don't know."
- "Why do you think she is behaving that way?" "I don't know."

"What" and "how" questions focus more on specifics and are less likely to be misunderstood, because they almost always imply a request for information. For example:

- "What, specifically, are your reasons for not going with me?"
  (The implied request is "Give me your rationale.")
- "What are you doing?"
  (The implied request is "Describe your behavior.")
- "How can I help her improve her behavior?"
  (The implied request is "Tell me some ways.")

Caution: Before using questions, ask yourself if there is any other way you can obtain the information or if there is another form of communication you can use. Many communication experts believe that we could probably communicate more effectively by cutting our use of questioning in half.

11. Utilize the power of silence and delayed response. Of all conflict response options, silence is the least understood yet potentially the most effective. *Strategic* use of silence can enable one to control the pace of most verbal interaction. By resisting the temptation to pack as many words as possible into our communication time, we can better manage emotionally loaded confrontations.

In normal conversations, the time between response is less than a second. As emotions heat up, the interresponse times diminish until interruption occurs more and more frequently and communication becomes impossible. By consciously waiting two, three, or four seconds before responding, you can stop verbal crowding and establish a more productive communication climate.

Caution: Considerable practice is necessary in overcoming the interruption habit, and care must be taken not to overuse silence. Sudden use of long periods of silence may cause confusion and increase hostility.

12. Do not be afraid to say, "You may be right." Acknowledging agreement where possible is an antidote to argument. When faced with resistance, try focusing on *any* point of agreement with your adversary. For example, say, "I agree with what you said about the production quotas" (area of agreement), *then* move on to the area of contention: "Now can you tell me more about how you feel about the way the work schedule is organized?"

If you cannot find anything substantive to agree about, agree with the other person's feelings. "I can see why you're angry, Bill.

It would gripe me too. Now how can we work this problem out?" It is remarkable how the phrase "You may be right" is almost magic in calming people down and creating a climate for listening.

An important lesson can be learned from Drucker's (1973) discussion of the trap of being right. He points out how the effective executive avoids it:[17]

> No matter how high his emotions run, no matter how certain he is that the other side is completely wrong and has no case at all, the executive who wants to make the right decision forces himself to see opposition as *his* means to think through the alternatives. He uses conflict of opinion as his tool to make sure all major aspects of an important matter are looked at carefully. (p. 475)

13. Avoid interpreting motives. Most of us are not perceptive, skilled, or well trained enough to interpret another's motivation. In conflict situations attempts at interpretation can be especially risky. Mind reading should be left to the experts. Avoid statements about another's behavior that have a "because" in them. Here are some examples.

I think you did that because:

● You wanted to hurt Mary.
● You are showing off your expertise.
● You feel inadequate.
● Your stomach hurts.

Such statements will only enrage the recipient. No one likes to be second guessed. It is more useful to accept what is said at face value and deal with it in whatever way is congruent with your values at that moment. This does not mean that you have to agree with it or like it; just avoid trying to guess what the other person is thinking.

14. Do not give advice. Advice is usually a well-meaning attempt to teach, preach, explain, command, or suggest. Under conditions of conflict, none of the above are needed, wanted, or appreciated. Even when conditions are serene and when advice is asked for, it is usually questioned, resisted, and hardly ever followed. To offer advice when faced with disagreement and opposition is to court disaster.

---

[17]Reprinted from P. Drucker. *Management.* New York: Harper & Row, 1973. Used with permission.

Another point to consider about giving advice is that it just might be followed. Then you would probably be held responsible if it did not work, thus prolonging the conflict.

HUMOR AND HOW IT CAN HELP
IF YOU ARE CAREFUL

Two facets of humor most useful in the management of conflict are (1) the possession of a *balanced* sense of humor based on optimism and good will and (2) the capacity for using humor *appropriately* when faced with difficult and demanding interpersonal encounters.

A balanced sense of humor depends on a philosophy of life that enables one to accept his or her own flaws and weaknesses without falling apart and to accept with equanimity the unfairness and changeability of life. Because most humor comes from pain, the ability to come to terms with the imperfections and ironies of life can be assisted by observing how people of wit have used humor in talking about things not easily talked about.

- Woody Allen on death: "I don't want to gain immortality through my work . . . I want to gain immortality by not dying."
- Voltaire on sex: "The pleasure is momentary, the position is ridiculous, and the expense is damnable."
- Groucho Marx on segregation: "I have this problem . . . I refuse to join a country club that would accept me as a member."
- John F. Kennedy on nepotism (when heavily criticized for appointing his brother Attorney General): "I see nothing wrong with giving Robert some legal experience as Attorney General before he goes out to practice law."

When asked in a television interview[18] how he was learning to deal with his changing appearance, his fear, and his pain, a courageous young cancer victim responded, "Instead of worrying about how I look, I laugh at myself in the mirror. Instead of worrying about anything, I laugh about it. It helps me." Children are often closer to humor than are adults. I have talked with many harassed school teachers who said that the only thing that kept them from quitting was that their job guaranteed them a few good laughs each day. Others said it another way: "What keeps me teaching is the fun I can have with the kids."

[18]Helpers. *Sixty Minutes.* CBS, December 9, 1979.

Humor is a personal buttress against the uncertainties of life. Pulitzer-Prize winner Rene Dubos (1974) said that the best protection against fate is to face life with a smile.

Appropriate use of humor in interpersonal conflict, however, requires more than a positively centered philosophy of life. It requires also an understanding of when to be funny in order to defuse tension and when not to. This calls for flawless timing and a great deal of intuitive common sense.

When it is your turn in the arena of conflict, the following suggestions may help:

1. Whether a participant or an arbitrator, be aware of your own perspective regarding the conflict. Look for the humor in the situation, but keep it to yourself. Examine words, body language, and expressions on faces. Is anything funny? This will help you keep your sense of balance, and perhaps an opportunity will come for appropriately injecting a little humor to break the tension.

2. Be aware of the social and behavioral norms of the person(s) in the conflict. For some, ridicule, wry responses, grim jokes, good-natured rudeness, and cynicism may be all right; but for others, such humor might be totally inappropriate. If it does not "feel" right, do not take a chance. A conflict situation is no place to experiment with humor.

3. Mentally exaggerate what is going on. Carry the exaggeration through to its ultimate absurdity. Exaggerate your feelings ("If this continues, I'll probably tear this contract up and scatter it all over the carpet. Then what will they think?") If it seems *appropriate,* ask a question that will allow another party to bring humor into play. For example, "Do you see anything ridiculous about what's going on here?" Exaggerate your own culpability in the conflict: For example, "I feel like a complete fool for doing this." "How could I have been stupid enough not to have seen that?" "This could ruin my entire life." or "We may have to put the children up for adoption." Exaggeration skillfully handled may sometimes break the tension and place things in proper perspective.

4. Turning a would-be tragedy into irony is another way to gain perspective. Compare catastrophic expectations with the minutiae of the here and now. Weller (1979) describes the difference between tragedy and irony in the words of Judith Viorst:[19]

---

[19]Reprinted from: S. Weller. Joseph Heller and Judith Viorst, Humor Can Save Your Life. *Self,* August 1979, pp. 46-51. Copyright © 1979 by The Conde Nast Publications Inc. Used with permission.

> Feeling something as tragedy is feeling your pain in a way that fills up the whole screen of your consciousness at the moment. Turning it into irony is shrinking it just enough so that you can also see all the other banal things that are going on in your life while you're in pain. Tragedy is: I'm bitterly disappointed and hurt, period. Irony is: I'm bitterly disappointed and hurt, and the cat's tail is caught in the door, and there's this smiling weatherman on the television screen talking about what a great day it is, and my mother calls and says, "Hello, dahling. Vat's new?" (p. 46)

Under the stress of conflict, the threat of what *may* happen will often contaminate the interaction going on at the moment. Irony helps keep things in the here and now.

5. Humor can be used to delay or postpone confrontation in an anger-filled situation that is going nowhere. Try saying something ludicrous about your inability to cope with what is happening. For example, "I think I need a graduate course in what not to say." "Hostility doesn't come easy for me; I think I'll need a little more practice before continuing." or "If things don't get better, I may have to stop helping." Try anything that fits the humor norms of the group in order to buy some time until everyone can regain poise.

6. Look for "human-condition" items that all parties may regard as funny. Because most people share common feelings of insecurity, anxiety, and anger, use an I-know-how-you-must-be-feeling type of humor by telling an anecdote about what happened to you the last time you were scared, angry, or insecure. The recognition of common predicaments is a powerful tension reducer.

Erma Bombeck (1979) wrote:

> After reading sixty-two books and articles on how to deal with oneself, I realized something was missing . . . a sense of humor. I cannot believe that people look into the mirror that reflects their actions and behavior and keep a straight face. (p. 255)

7. Make sure your nonverbal signals match your humorous intent. Congruency between your words and nonverbal behavior is necessary for humor to be an effective conflict-defusion strategy. Appropriate facial clues and body postures must accompany a light-hearted "kidding" approach in order to avoid any implication of sarcasm, denigration, or put down. Whenever someone's nonverbal message contradicts the verbal message, it is the former that will be perceived, and nonproductive confrontation will probably increase.

In keeping with these suggestions, humor in conflict is best used:

- To break through the rigidity, pomposity, and overseriousness generated by heavy ego involvement;
- To make people laugh so that they will feel better physically; and
- To create a togetherness by laughing *with* each other rather than a separation by laughing *at* each other.

Summary:

- It is *usually* O.K. to poke fun at yourself.
- It is *sometimes* O.K. to make fun of the situation (as in exaggeration).
- It is *extremely risky* to make light of someone else; the more potentially volatile the conflict, the greater the risk.
- Do not feel compelled to use humor; it is only one of many options.
- Go with your own style and your visceral intelligence.
- When in doubt, do not use humor.

HOW TO DEAL WITH POTENTIALLY VIOLENT CONFLICT

Each day the media offer increasingly frightening descriptions of how rapidly physical violence can become the ugly by-product of interpersonal conflict. Even less comforting is the statistical evidence that we are more likely to be assaulted by friends or relatives than by strangers. Although it is outside the scope of this book to deal with physical self-defense,[20] there are some specific practices that can help minimize risk in dangerous situations that have not degenerated into physical violence.

Literature about previolent behavior—although somewhat helpful at a theoretical level—offers few practical suggestions about how to prepare for those ugly situations that we hope never

---

[20]Libraries and bookstores contain many self-help books about self-defense. Additional information about personal protection from violent action may be obtained from a variety of sources, such as local law-enforcement agencies, YMCA, YWCA, colleges, universities, adult schools, and many private and nonprofit organizations.

happen. The disappointing lack of useful information about this topic prompted me to seek suggestions and opinions from people whose jobs place them in continuous contact with previolent and violent behavior. My "research" was simple. I asked three basic questions of an array of law-enforcement officers, crisis counselors, psychiatrists, psychologists, selected educators, and other effective and skilled professionals. The three questions were:

1. How do you recognize a potentially violent interpersonal conflict? (Recognition)
2. How do you get yourself ready to deal with the possibility of violence? (Readiness)
3. What practices do you use to prevent escalation into violence? (Prevention)

The responses that reflect the greatest unanimity are presented here for your consideration, but you must be the judge of whether or not they fit your style (remember Chapter 2).

Recognition: How To Recognize Potential Violence

1. Rely on your visceral intelligence. If a situation does not "feel" right and the hairs on the back of your neck are standing at attention or if the "vibrations" all spell trouble, do not take chances. We all have fairly reliable instinct and intuition—if we pay attention to it. Of course, the more experience you have had with violence, the more likely you will "call" it accurately.

2. Read the nonverbal behavior. Body posture, tone of voice, etc. (see "Pay attention to the music" in this chapter), are far better indicators than the words being used.[21] Look for undue agitation, tight lips, clenched fists, flared nostrils, wide-open eyes, and other obvious signs of emotional short circuits.

3. Study the history. Has this person or group had a history of violence? If you do not know the person or group, find out what you can from others before confronting.

4. Be aware of the onlookers. People on the scene may either inhibit or provoke violence. The need to show off or prove something may escalate a problem. On the other hand, an audience may restrict conflict to civilized conversation. Use this to your advantage.

---

[21]There are technical exceptions; for example, gang-related word cues or gestures that trigger premeditated assaults.

5. Look for evidence of psychic modifiers. Alcohol, drugs, and other mind-bending substances or practices make conflict situations extremely unpredictable and uncontrollable. "Get help or get out" and "Never try to reason with a drunk or a user" were often-repeated pieces of advice.

Readiness: How To Prepare Yourself for Potential Violence

1. Slow down. Talk gently to yourself. Breathe deeply and slowly. Exaggerate the desensitization and self-control strategies outlined at the beginning of this chapter.

2. Mentally design a safety plan. Take precautions regarding what to do if the situation becomes dangerous. Check out the environment for a graceful or convenient exit or for possible sources of assistance.

3. Play the options game. Think of as many alternatives as you can for resolving the situation. This mental exercise may give you a sense of control and will usually calm you down.

4. Expect anything. It helps to appear "unsurprisable," especially if you are the target of abusive language. No matter how offensive it is, tell yourself you have heard it all.

5. Respect the other person(s). If you convince yourself that your adversary is doing exactly what he or she needs to do, given his or her perception of reality, your ego is not as likely to cause you to escalate the situation. *Force* yourself to perceive the event with as much detachment as possible. This will give you a decided edge, and your good will may even be reciprocated.

Prevention: How To Reduce the Possibility of Violence

1. Maintain nonthreatening body posture. About a twenty-degree angle from direct confrontation while maintaining friendly nonchallenging eye contact is a good stance. Be careful not to crowd the other person's comfort zone. Stay at least two feet away.

2. Speak with a calm, firm, and soothing tone. An unhurried rate of conversation will also help. Adequate intervals between verbal exchanges will sometimes help reduce anxiety. (The use of silence was discussed earlier in this chapter.) Avoid trigger words or threatening language.

3. Avoid touching a potentially violent person. Physical contact *may* help, but it is extremely risky and is more apt to provoke violence. A large number of assaults on teachers have been triggered by touching angry or anxious students.

4. *Suggest moving to a spacious location.* Physical movement and spacious surroundings sometimes have a calming effect on upset people.

5. *Attend totally to the person you are working with.* Concentrate on the here and now and avoid thinking about the issue to be resolved, about what went on in the past, or about what may happen in the future. Attend to the moment. When dealing with potential violence, it becomes a matter of *de-escalating,* not problem solving. If you allow your mind to wander too far away from present behavior, you may either intimidate yourself or miss important opportunities for de-escalation.

6. *Do not attempt mind reading.* People about to become violent have very complex reasons for behaving the way they do. Unless you have had much training or experience, trying to figure out their motives will probably not help much and may be distracting. Just look, listen, and deal with what you see and hear on the surface.

7. *Use distraction to defuse violent energy.* Any kind of appropriate distraction will provide a break in the tension. For example:

- Make a request; ask for a small favor, such as the time, a pen, a light, or anything that temporarily refocuses the negative energy.
- Make an "off-the-wall" comment. Say something that has nothing to do with the current conflict, such as "Do you smell something burning?" This seemingly inappropriate behavior may interrupt the hostile mood of the moment. Acting out of character may produce a totally different response in a previolent person.
- Act confused or deliberately make a stupid statement about the conflict. This may cause a previolent person to explain things to you. Such "explaining" may defuse some anger.

8. *Use a graduated response system.* In attempting defusion or de-escalation of a conflict, begin with the lower risk, least-aggressive methods. You can always escalate, but it is almost impossible to back away from a hard-line position. Consider force only for self-protection. Ask yourself, "What are the likely consequences of initiating physical force?" This is particularly important if you are in conflict with a stranger or someone who may be under the influence of drugs. Consider the fact that it sometimes takes four or five police officers to subdue a 130-pound fifteen-year-old who is high on PCP.

9. *Here are some high risk methods to try when all else fails:*

- Appropriate humor may work if you have the style, confidence, and credibility to pull it off (see the section on using humor). However, attempts at being funny in previolent situations may have serious consequences if misinterpreted.

- Under certain conditions, hard-shock methods—such as yelling and using words like "stop," "shut up," or "that's enough"—may startle the person and prevent escalation, but they are risky.

- In rare cases, dire predictions—such as "Someone's going to get hurt" or "Do you want to end up in jail?"—may interrupt the action long enough for the person to regain some poise.

10. *Leave gracefully.* After exhausting all of your resources and getting nowhere, leave the scene with as much dignity as you can muster. You have done the best you can, and it is now time to protect yourself.

These twenty ideas for handling previolent conflicts carry no guarantees of success. They are only composite suggestions of some practicing professionals. Under certain conditions they may also work for you.

COMMENT

We have covered a lot of territory in Chapter 4, and you cannot expect to read it through swiftly and then recall every point at just the right moment in a conflict situation. After you have read the chapter carefully and understand its message, go back and select a section that you especially need or that you are especially interested in or concerned about. Within that section, select the methods that seem suitable for you and role play the part—at least mentally. When you feel comfortable with your new role, try it in real situations. Then select another area of the chapter and repeat the learning process.

Chapter 5

How To Use Power and Problem Solving in Managing Conflict

Self-reverence, self-knowledge, self-control,
These three alone lead life to sovereign power.

Tennyson
in Oenone

The measure of man is what he does with power.

Pittacus

Probably the most universally recommended strategies for managing conflict involve using power and solving problems. Organizational, developmental, management-training, and self-help literature are replete with suggestions about how to use power and how to solve problems, yet such suggestions have limited practical value unless a person has sharp awareness of his or her feelings and beliefs about each strategy. For example, the following kinds of questions must be addressed: Is the use of power always negative or coercive? Is problem solving the only civilized way to approach conflict? Am I willing to risk what it takes to use power? Am I willing to spend the time involved in problem-solving approaches to conflict? Recipes alone are not enough: the recipes or suggestions must be processed and assimilated by each person who expects to use them.

Power and problem solving are emphasized in this chapter to reinforce the thesis of this book, which contends that the method of managing conflict is not nearly as important as is the degree to which that method is integrated in each user's unique situation. Furthermore, the user's perception of the method should correspond with his or her style. It is precisely because conflict is unstable and volatile that the integrity provided by this inside-out approach becomes necessary to the conflict manager—especially when he or she contemplates the use of power.

POWER AND CONFLICT

Think about the following perceptions of power and how they might influence one's approach to interpersonal conflict.

- Power: "the possession of control, authority, or influence over others" (*Webster's New Collegiate Dictionary*).

- "All life is a game of power. The object of the game is simple enough; to know what you want and get it" (Korda, 1975, p. 4).

- "Punishments and rewards are the sources from which a person's power is derived" (Gordon, 1977, p. 156).

- "When your consciousness is focused on power you are concerned with dominating people and situations, increasing prestige, wealth and pride in addition to thousands of more subtle forms of hierarchy, manipulation and control" (Keyes, 1973, p. 59).

- "The paradox [of power] is that you have tremendous control over your life, but you give up that control when you try to control others. For the only way you can control others is to recognize their natures and do what is necessary to evoke the desired reactions from those natures. Thus, your actions are dictated by the requirements involved when you attempt to control someone else" (Browne, 1975, p. 26).[22]

How do you perceive power? As control *over* someone? As some kind of internal strength? As both? As neither? As something entirely different? Whatever it is, your view will significantly affect the way you handle conflicts, because most conflicts are power transactions.

Here is another way to think about it. Take a moment and reflect on these questions: Who do you think of when you think of a "powerful" person? What makes that person powerful? Write your thoughts here: _____

_____

_____
_____

[22]Reprinted from Harry Browne. *How I Found Freedom in an Unfree World.* New York: Avon, 1975. Copyright © 1973 by Harry Browne. Used with permission.

The use of power per se is neither good nor bad. To the question, "How should power be used in conflict?" the caveat "It depends" must apply. Popular books on power range in philosophy from Ringer's (1979) *Winning Through Intimidation,* which suggests coercive dog-eat-dog strategies, to Gordon's (1980) *Leader Effectiveness Training,* which forbids the use of coercive power. As usual, somewhere in the middle lies the truth.

A large part of that truth is related to the kinds of power that we have at our disposal and that we bring to bear either consciously or unconsciously in conflicts and confrontations. No one is powerless. Review the following categories and suggestions, and then make some decisions about *your* power resources.

Natural Power. Natural power may be derived from personal attributes, such as physical beauty, size, strength, energy, verbal fluency, intelligence, and wisdom, which—when scrambled together—give that person "presence," "likeability," or "charisma." These intangibles are not often discussed (perhaps because they are difficult to measure), but they can be the most influential factors in conflict situations. Make a list of your strengths in this category. Make another list of the natural-power attributes of others to which you are most vulnerable (e.g., intelligence or beauty).

My Natural-Power Attributes	*Influential Natural-Power Attributes of Others*
_____	_____
_____	_____
_____	_____
_____	_____
_____	_____
_____	_____

Acquired Power. This power is obtained by studying; working hard; acquiring knowledge, skill, and information; and consciously cultivating your reputation and credibility. It can be called the power of expertise. It is what inspires awe of doctors, lawyers, and plumbers, and it is what enables most shop teachers in schools to have fewer discipline problems than other teachers. Acquired expert power comes from knowing or being able to do something useful that others do not know or cannot do. How are you doing in this category? What expertise do you have that gives you power in certain situations? Note these strengths here:

_____

_____

_____

_____

_____

Top-Dog or Parent Power. This is the power of domination that accompanies social or financial status or is conferred by a chain of command in an organization. This power has great potential for rewarding and punishing. It is the most often abused, resented, and resisted. Make some notes about the ways you use or abuse your authority or status.

_____

_____

_____

_____

_____

Force or Coercive Power. This power mode is often chosen because it implies strength and decisiveness. Although force and coercion *may* be effective under some conditions, in conflict situations it is risky and unpredictable at best. If you choose to use it or can think of no other option, the following suggestions may help cut your losses.

1. Be certain that what you do feels comfortable and looks like it fits you. Nothing is as ludicrous as behavior that is incongruent with that person's personality or style. For example, one workshop leader attempted an assertiveness role play with a workshop participant who had such a commanding personal presence that he made the leader look like a hapless pip-squeak. The assertive behavior did not fit either the leader's image or the situation. It was like a battle between someone who had completed the first three lessons in a YMCA karate class and an experienced street fighter in a dark alley.

2. Exercise extreme care in attempting to *overpower* an adversary in a win-lose conflict. Like Pyrrhus,[23] the cost may be too high. You may win the battle and lose the war—as did the employee who "proved" to his boss that he was right and later lost his job or the spouse who continually won all the arguments and as a prize received a divorce. Force may serve only to begin another conflict.

3. Only use the power of force or coercion when you have what it takes to back it up. Be sure that you have the authority, respect, charisma, stamina, or whatever else is needed to enforce the decision. Force usually requires continuous vigilance and maintenance. For example, if I punish (overpower) my son by restricting his freedom to leave the house, I must enforce the restriction. This may mean that I, too, will have to stay home when I prefer to go out, and I may not be willing to pay that price. Bosses who run their operations through coercion have similar problems. In each conflict they must maintain the fear system that gives them power.

4. Before using force or coercion in conflict, you should ask yourself, "Does it work for me? Can I use it and stay physically and emotionally healthy?"

---

[23]Pyrrhus, a Greek king who lived between 318 and 272 B.C., was a skillful warrior who fought intensely against the Romans. His military successes were so costly that he eventually had to give up and return to Greece; hence the term "Pyrrhic victory."

Describe an instance in which you saw force or coercive power backfire on the user.

_____

_____

_____

_____

Underdog or "Helpless" Power. This is the subtle and poorly understood power of helplessness and destructive manipulation through behaviors that resist, divert, and delay. In this category can be found most of the behaviors that induce guilt. Dreikurs (1957) classifies helplessness as the most tyrannical power that a child can use on adults. Nevertheless, adults also use it on each other. Gestalt psychologists often refer to the power inherent in the "underdog" position. Dreikurs suggests some interesting ways to handle this strategy.

Have you used this kind of power or had it used on you? Give some of the details.

_____

_____

_____

_____

Independence Power. This power position is achieved when we become relatively independent of other people for gratification of our needs. We are controlled by others in conflicts only when they control something we want, such as status, wealth, freedom, or sexual gratification. If, for example, you are a boss and your subordinate tells you what you can do with the job, you have no power over that subordinate. The same applies when an attempt is made to punish children by taking away privileges that they do not care about. To paraphrase Thoreau, we are powerful in proportion to what we can do without.

How much independence do you have in your work life and home life? Not enough? Too much? How does this affect you in conflict situations?

_____

_____

_____

_____

_____

The Power of Interdependence. We are never more alone than when embroiled in interpersonal conflict and faced with hostility and opposition. Under such conditions, our vulnerability increases dramatically as we question our ability to cope, abandon our self-confidence, and intimidate ourselves in all kinds of creative ways. Fortunately, the power to deal with troubling conflicts can be bolstered by those special people whom we can consistently count on. Those who give us active support and counsel and those whom we can trust to back us up in our decisions provide a certain security and strength that can be referred to as the "power of interdependence."

Who are the people in your life on whom you can really depend? To whom can you turn when you are dealing with the loneliness of conflict? Do you reciprocate and work at maintaining your relationships with these supporters? (For more on this topic, see "Developing and Nurturing Support Systems" in Chapter 7.)

_____

_____

_____

The Power of Self-Confidence. As our skills in dealing with conflict begin to bring us success we develop the most important kind of power: self-confidence. This is the power that helps us confront and manage conflict in ways that enable us to feel good without having to make someone else feel bad. When you have self-confidence in a conflict situation, both parties benefit, because self-confidence is the antithesis of the insecurity that often causes destructive behavior and prolongs animosity.

The following inventory has been used often by individuals and groups to assess their confidence and personal power.

Directions:

1. Write a brief response to the question(s) under each item. (It may help to keep in mind a particular reference group, e.g., co-workers, family, employees, bosses, or social acquaintances.)

2. Circle a number on the continuum that best corresponds with your view of yourself and make a few notes pertinent to the topic. Write whatever enters your mind.

3. Review the work sheet and locate the areas in which you feel least confident or least powerful.

4. Ask a few people whom you trust and whom you know well to answer—on unused inventory forms—the questions as *they* perceive you. This is a valuable source of information about yourself, because it is often difficult to evaluate your own impact on others.

5. If your "soft spots" are validated, think about some ways to work on them. Talk to your collaborators and listen to their suggestions. Press them for behaviorally specific advice.

Personal Power and Confidence Inventory

1. *Physical Appearance and Vitality*
   How do I feel about my appearance when working or socializing with others? _____

   _____

1	2	3	4	5	6	7	8	9	10
always negatively									always positively

notes: _____

_____

_____

2. *Body Usage*
   What kind of image do I project by the way I carry myself and
   make eye contact? _____

   _____

1	2	3	4	5	6	7	8	9	10

   weak and   strong and
   negative   positive

   notes: _____

   _____

   _____

3. *Voice Quality*
   How effectively do I use my voice in tone, inflection, and
   volume? _____

   _____

1	2	3	4	5	6	7	8	9	10

   ineffectively   effectively

   notes: _____

   _____

   _____

4. *Symbolism*

What image do I present to others regarding the way I am groomed, my clothes and jewelry, what I carry, etc.? Are these things consistently appropriate? _____

_____

1	2	3	4	5	6	7	8	9	10

inappropriate   appropriate

notes: _____

_____

_____

5. *Sensitivity*

How well can I "read" or sense others? _____

_____

1	2	3	4	5	6	7	8	9	10

usually   extremely
inaccurately   accurately

notes: _____

_____

_____

6. *Status*

How do I feel about my organizational, social, or financial status? _____

_____

1	2	3	4	5	6	7	8	9	10

unsure   sure and
or shaky   stable

notes: _____

_____

_____

7. *Knowledge and Skills*
   How secure do I feel about what I am doing or talking about?

   _____

   _____

   | 1 | 2 | 3 | 4 | 5 | 6 | 7 | 8 | 9 | 10 |

   very   almost
   insecure   always secure

   notes: _____

   _____

   _____

8. *Past Successes*
   What kind of success record do I have for accomplishing
   whatever I attempt? _____

   _____

   | 1 | 2 | 3 | 4 | 5 | 6 | 7 | 8 | 9 | 10 |

   poor   excellent

   notes: _____

   _____

   _____

9. *Support*

How do I feel about the support I receive from the people with whom I spend most of my time? Do I feel that they are usually with me or against me? _____

_____

1	2	3	4	5	6	7	8	9	10

usually uncertain   certain and
or weak   strong

notes: _____

_____

_____

10. *Charisma*

What is my assessment of my personal power in affecting people, individually or in groups? _____

_____

1	2	3	4	5	6	7	8	9	10

weak   strong

notes: _____

_____

_____

By working carefully through this survey, you will begin to get in touch with your power and confidence as well as areas of vulnerability. This is the type of information that needs to be pondered and discussed with your colleagues or with your support network. Then you should select one or two areas and experiment with some specific behavioral changes, e.g., use the mirror, the tape recorder, and other people. Check again some of the suggestions in "Pathway 2" in Chapter 2. Work on your "soft spots" in nonthreatening situations before using them in hostile environments.

PROBLEM SOLVING AND CONFLICT

During the past decade, an important part of human relations and organization development training has been "win-win" conflict management. The purpose of this specialized training has been to deal with interpersonal differences in cooperative, collaborative, and compromising ways so that mutually acceptable solutions can be developed and no one will "lose." As laudable as this objective may be, it is extremely difficult to achieve, because for most of us "win-win" methods seem *unnatural.* We have been conditioned for years to react to conflict situations as battles to be won rather than as problems to be solved. Our socialization is based in great part on competition. Winners are rewarded in sports, business, and all other phases of our culture. Losers are, at best, ignored and, at worst, punished. Within this ambience it is difficult to turn off the win-lose competitive urge when faced with interpersonal conflicts even though the overwhelming evidence indicates that collaborative problem solving is more fruitful.

In spite of this competitive conditioning, there are those among us (let us call them "positive problem solvers") who regard conflicting differences in values, needs, and emotional disposition as natural events to be managed as humanely as possible. If you have ever had the good fortune of living or working with one of these rare people, you know what a joy it can be. If you happen to be such a person, read no farther. However, in case you would like to develop a more rewarding style of handling your conflicts, here are two suggestions.

Suggestion 1:
Practice Problem-Centered Self-Talk

If you recorded on paper or tape all the conversations that take place in your mind, you could probably fill several volumes a week. This internal dialog helps us figure things out and is a precursor to action. Therefore, what we say to ourselves about difficult situations in which we may find ourselves is extremely important. When confronted with unpredictable and unpleasant conflicts, we can easily slip into unproductive self-talk such as:

- "Oh, my God, what's going to happen now?"
- "They're doing it to me again."
- "I just can't face this."

- "Why me?"
- "I'll show them. I'll . . . "

This self-talk will only increase your anxiety as well as your chances for doing something inappropriate. Instead, try sending the following problem-focused messages to yourself.

Self-Talk Message 1. "This is a situation that needs careful attention. How can I (we) work it out?"

Use whatever variation of these words you wish, such as "What can I do about this problem now?" or "How can we both get what we want?" The important point is to get the message across to yourself that this is not a cause for panic; it can be worked out. Resist letting negative dialog seep in.

Self-Talk Message 2. "There is always something I (we) can do that will work better than this mess we're in now."

Continue to talk to yourself about your options rather than about catastrophic expectations. This will keep you open to creative opportunities for workable compromise.

Self-Talk Message 3. "They [whomever you are in conflict with] are doing exactly what *they* need to do. I can control only what I do."

Emphasis here is that by working on yourself you can influence others. It keeps you away from nonproductive self-talk, such as "They've got to stop that." "Why can't they see how wrong they are?" or "I'll *make* them do it." This message helps you avoid the trap of trying to change the other person; something that can only be done (temporarily) with a loaded gun or its equivalent. Problem-centered self-talk requires practice. Every chance you have, whether the conflict is large or small, continue to recycle the three messages through your brain:

- How can we work it out?
- There are always options.
- I can control only what *I* do.

This process conditions you to break out of ego-dominated and anxiety-producing patterns of self-intimidation or attempts to overpower others. Such conditioning will help keep you away from the panic or depression that comes from feeling that your options are closed and that there is no way out. The idea is to keep yourself positively oriented until your conflict adversary is ready to work on the situation as a *problem* rather than a *contest*.

Suggestion 2:
Practice the Basics of Interpersonal Problem Solving

Among the hundreds of existing problem-solving systems, certain common elements are useful in managing conflict. The following problem-solving sequence may be used unilaterally as you work out the conflict for yourself or in cooperation with your adversaries—*if* they agree to work with you.[24]

Step 1: Define the problem. All problem-solving systems start with defining and identifying issues (and nonissues), hence the old adage, "Once a problem is properly defined, it is half solved." It is at this point that we smoke out the issues by asking questions such as:

- "What's happening here?"
- "Is this a real problem or isn't it?"
- "If the problem is real, who owns it?"
- "Why do I need to take action?"

It is sometimes helpful to write down the issues on a "what's-happening" list as they occur to you. Let us examine a conflict between Bill and Jenny, married ten years. They have two children, ages eight and five. Bill's work requires long and frequently irregular hours. Jenny works part time but has a flexible schedule that she can control. She has a strong desire to keep the family on a regular routine and feels that this is important to the security of the children. For Jenny, an important part of this routine is the evening meal. It upsets her when Bill does not come home for dinner. This situation has become a constant source of aggravation leading to frequent quarrels and some unpleasant scenes. As the arguments increase, so do Bill's absences.

Jenny and Bill's "what's-happening" list might look like this:

- Bill sometimes has to respond to job demands that are not predictable. He misses dinner or is late two or three times a week.
- Jenny expects Bill to be home on time unless he calls. When Bill is late, he always calls but sometimes not until dinner is on the table.
- Jenny often eats alone with the children.

---

[24]How to convince an adversary to enter into collaborative problem solving will depend on your relationship, the existing situation, and your effective use of all previously suggested strategies plus a little luck.

- Arguments are occurring about three times per week with increasing vehemence.
- Jenny feels resentful.
- Bill feels guilty, frustrated, and angry.
- Both Jenny and Bill are concerned about the effect of this conflict on the children. Both see their relationship at an all-time low as reflected by their rapidly deteriorating sex life.

The list should reflect everything significant that is happening in any given situation. Next make a second list for the way you would like things to be. In the case of two or more people, each person should make his or her own list, and then they should be compiled. Jenny's and Bill's "the-way-it-should-be" lists included:

- Time for the family to be together regularly, preferably at dinner (from Jenny's list).
- Family adaptation to Bill's irregular work schedule (from Bill's list).
- Fewer arguments and personal attacks (from both lists).
- Less tension and disruption in the home (from both lists).

There is something about writing things down that helps to clarify situations and place points of contention in proper perspective. When you have all of your "would-like-to-have-happen" items in front of you, it is important to question each one by asking "why?" "Why is dinner together so important?" "Why do we want fewer arguments?" "If dinner were always attended regularly, would we argue about something else?" By answering these questions you will also do three other things:

- Smoke out issues that may be hidden, disguised, or dormant.
- Increase the chances that you are working on the right problem.
- Discover who really "owns" the problem, i.e., who is experiencing the most discomfort in the conflict situation. In the case of Jenny and Bill, this process helped them discover that it was not so much the dinner issue as it was some strong feelings about family togetherness stemming from Jenny's background as a foster child.

Step 2: State clearly what you think. Making a clear and "official" statement about what is wanted focuses energy on something tangible that can be worked on. The statement should be general enough to enable you to explore as broad a range of options as possible. In the example of Jenny and Bill, the statement about wanting to cut down on arguments and reduce tensions surfaced as more important than the more narrow objective of being together at dinner.

Step 3: Generate possible solutions. An effective way to generate solutions is a modified brainstorming process. First each party spends about five minutes in writing down as many solutions to the problem as possible. The ideas do not have to be logical. At this point quantity, not quality, is important. If you are working on the conflict by yourself, you may ask some creative people to help you brainstorm.

If several parties to the conflict are working in collaboration, the second step is to pool the lists into a master list and to spend some time adding and/or combining ideas. No judging or logical evaluation should be attempted at this point.

Third, the nonworkable ideas (as determined by consensus) are discarded and the others are examined.

Fourth, priorities—based on criteria essential to what the parties want to achieve (from Step 2)—are assigned to the remaining items. The longer the lists, the greater the possibilities for resolving the conflict.

These are the items (in priority order) that Jenny and Bill left on their list at the conclusion of their search for solutions:

1. Arrange for at least one-half hour of uninterrupted time each day to "talk things over."
2. Work out an agreement on some "rules" for discussing sensitive items.
3. Do not allow resentment and anger to build up.
4. Avoid surprising each other with bad news.
5. Take the kids out to dinner at least once every two weeks at a restaurant near Bill's office.
6. Kiss and hold each other before talking whenever we have not seen each other all day.

The items on the priority list are not nearly as important as the fact that they went through the process and now have some joint ownership in the plan.

Step 4: Reality test each solution. Apply the following reality test to each item on your priority list.

- Is there common understanding of the idea? Do we have the same perception of what it means?
- Is it realistically possible to accomplish?
- Do we have the necessary desire and commitment to make it work?
- What are all the possible things that could go wrong with the idea? What will happen if we try it and it does not work?

You may think of other questions that will help you anticipate the possible success or failure of your conflict-management plan.

Step 5: Make a "what-if" contingency plan. Before taking action, decide what your procedure will be if your plan does not work. If you are working by yourself, think about some options you might want to exercise. If it is a collaborative conflict-management effort, agree on how to renegotiate if things do not work out as planned. (See the section on negotiation in Chapter 3.)

Step 6: Do it. Put your plan into action with a built-in agreement to re-evaluate it and see how it is going within a reasonable time.

The conflict problem-solving process used in the preceding home-life example can also be applied to the management of organizational or work-life conflicts between a supervisor and employee(s), competing colleagues, departments, etc. Simply use the following work sheet formally or informally for working through the process.

Conflict Problem-Solving Work Sheet

1. *Definition of the Problem:*
   What is happening here?

   My list   Your list

   _____   _____

   _____   _____

   _____   _____

   _____   _____

Whose problem is it? (Clear up differences in perception here.)

I say	You say
_____	_____
_____	_____
_____	_____
_____	_____

How would I (we) like things to be?

My list	Your list
_____	_____
_____	_____
_____	_____
_____	_____

Why do I (we) have to take action? What would happen if we did nothing?

I say	You say
_____	_____
_____	_____
_____	_____
_____	_____

2. *Official Statement(s):*

What is my (our) clearest statement of what I (we) want? (Check statements to see if they reflect mutual understanding of the conflict or problem.)

My statement   Your statement

_____   _____

_____   _____

_____   _____

_____   _____

_____

3. *Possible Solutions:*

(Work these out individually without talking; then share and prioritize them together.) What are all the possible solutions to the problem (in priority order)?

1. _____

2. _____

3. _____

4. _____

5. _____

6. _____

7. _____

8. _____

4. *Reality Test:*

Reality test each solution against these questions. Start with the highest priority and work down.

- Is there common understanding of the idea? Do we have the same perception of what it means?
- Is it realistically possible to accomplish?
- Do we have the necessary desire and commitment to make it work?
- What are all the possible things that could go wrong with the idea? What will happen if we try it and it does not work?

5. *Contingency Plan:*

What will be "Plan B" if the first plan does not work? (Agree on how to renegotiate.)

_____

_____

_____

_____

_____

_____

_____

_____

6. *Action:*
   Carry out your best (highest priority) solution in small, agreed-on, realistic steps to enhance possibilities for success. Build in an agreement to re-evaluate the solution within a reasonable time and to plan again if necessary.

Going It Alone

The problem-solving process has thus far been based on the presumption that all parties to the conflict have been operating in good faith with a sincere desire to solve the problem. Now let us deal with the question of what to do when the people with whom you are in conflict are not interested in your good ideas about problem solving. They want to win and do not care whether or not they run over you in the process. They are playing win-lose when you want to play win-win. This may well happen, because conflict caused by personality factors is often not amenable to management by problem solving. How can you take care of yourself under such conflict conditions?

First, remember that you cannot change others, so continue your positive self-talk. It will help keep you centered and help reduce anxiety. Next, go through exactly the same problem-solving procedure with a slightly different focus. You are now using the process unilaterally to figure out how best to take care of *yourself* in this conflict:

- Define your problem;
- State (to yourself) what you want;
- Generate as many ideas as possible;
- Reality test each idea and select the best ones;
- Make a contingency plan; and
- Act on your best option.

Finally, keep reminding yourself that although there are no pat answers, you are never without options. This is critically important because of the correlation between limited options and anxiety. The fewer the perceived options, the higher the stress level. That one can always make choices, even under the most difficult conditions, was eloquently pointed out in Frankl's (1959) moving account of survival in the Nazi death camps during World War II.

As long as you are alive you can make choices that are independent of others. The final human options in almost any situation are to stay, to go, or to change.

COMMENT

Even when you use power in managing conflict, you can still view the situation as a problem to be solved. Problem-solving tactics can be used to decide whether or not power can or should be employed and, if so, what type of power and to what extent. Power can also be used to influence the other party to view the conflict as a problem to be solved. Therefore, whether a conflict requires primary use of power or problem solving, the other tactic can be used as a secondary method.

Chapter 6

How To Help Others Handle Conflict (or Being an Effective Third Party)

Against a foe I can myself defend—
But Heaven protect me
From a blundering friend.

D'Arcy W. Thompson

Among the many demands of life for which we are untrained, interpersonal peacemaking is perhaps the one for which we are least prepared. Nevertheless, as parents, friends, lovers, family members, bosses, colleagues, and a host of other roles, we continually find ourselves in situations requiring that we help others work out their conflicts. For example, you may become involved in the following situations:

- At work, two people in the unit for which you have responsibility are in such persistent disagreement that performance is in a tailspin. You need to take action.

- Your church group has asked you to help work through a political power struggle about the new pastor. This issue has split the membership and threatens the health of the entire organization.

- Although a hard-driving sales manager, who works for you, consistently meets or exceeds her budget, she is pushing the sales force too hard. This method is producing results, but the hassles and subtle resistances are increasing. You have received several indications that not all is well. The sales manager fails to see the problem and points to her successful record.

- Three of the most effective managers who report to you are competing for a promotion and are using destructive tactics that go beyond healthy competition. Something must be done.

- As a junior-high-school administrator, you are concerned because a neighborhood dispute among several families has spilled over into the classrooms, disrupting an atmosphere that is conducive to learning.

- While dining with two of your closest colleagues, they become involved in a violent argument. This is not the first time this has happened. After all the dirty laundry has been aired, they calm down and turn to you for advice. You feel the need to do something.

If more examples would only increase your feelings of apprehension about serving as a helper or mediator, do not be discouraged. Many trained professionals have similar concerns about mediating conflict, largely because so little practical training in this field is available. We can, however, learn much from the peacemaking professions connected with national and international politics, organization development, labor relations, law enforcement, crisis counseling, psychology, social work, and related areas. Each of these professions has its own game rules and specialized procedures for dealing with human behavior in conflict situations. From these procedures,[25] certain powerful peacemaking concepts can be incorporated into our common sense and adapted to our use when we are faced with the task of informally mediating interpersonal disputes.

WHAT TO DO BEFORE BECOMING INVOLVED

It is both tempting and flattering to be asked to intercede to help people to "work things out." How nurturing to one's ego to be thought of as wise, skilled, reliable, and trusted! Who could turn down such an offer? On the other hand, think about the enormous responsibility of interfering in the lives of others, magnified by the possibility that a clumsy third-party intervention could turn almost any minor conflict into a disaster. If you have a choice about whether or not to become involved, consider these questions.

Do you have the personal resources to help improve the conflict situation? For example: a modicum of skills and experience in communication and conflict management—skills such as the ones described in previous sections of this book; some credibility with the people you are trying to help (i.e., they know you,

---

[25]Should you wish to examine some useful and informative references, consult Karras (1970, 1974) and Nierenberg (1968).

trust you, and respect you to a reasonable extent); the time and energy to stay with the situation and follow through as needed; and the sensitivity and intuition that this conflict may demand.

Is it too late to be of assistance? Often conflicts reach a point of no return, a point at which it appears that both positions have become fixed in concrete. In such cases no amount of help will do any good and it is better to let the scenario run its course. Intervening in such cases would probably waste everyone's time and expose you to frustration and disappointment.

Could they work it out better without you? This is a very important question. Are you being asked to help in order to give the disputants an easy way out? Have the parties spent enough time trying to handle their disagreement before asking a third party? Do you have a lot of power over one or both parties? If so, your value as a third party may be compromised.

Do both parties want you to help? Are you being drawn into a no-win situation? Avoid being trapped by one party who *unilaterally* requests third-party help in order to gain an advantage. Make sure *all* parties to the conflict want your help.

Does it "feel" right to become involved? What are your instincts telling you? What are the chances for success? After reasoning out all of the pros and cons of involvement, allow your intuition to make the final decision.

WHAT TO DO AFTER YOU DECIDE TO HELP

Recognize your power and your vulnerability. When you are invited in good faith to help manage a conflict, you are in a power position. Use the power judiciously. You are entitled to make some demands about conditions under which you will or will not help. You can set some ground rules and request that you be given a reasonable amount of control in order to facilitate communication. Consider the possibility that if things do not work out well, you may be blamed by one or both parties. Third parties make convenient scapegoats.

Use one-on-one discussions to obtain a more accurate picture of the conflict. Talking privately with each party will help determine that person's perception of the dispute and may well smoke out some hidden agendas. One-on-one conversations not only provide useful information to the third party, but will also help prepare the disputants for confrontations. Meeting with the third party in advance tends to take some of the anxiety out of the first three-way confrontation.

Balance the power of the disputants. In almost all conflicts there is a power disparity between the parties. One is invariably weaker, less capable, or less influential than the other. A basic third-party service is to equalize the power. The easiest way to do this is to establish ground rules that will ensure that each person receives a fair share of air time, that each position is adequately heard by the other party (see the section on conflict communication in Chapter 4), and that no recriminations are experienced. Keep the ground rules simple but firm and intervene as often as necessary to ensure adherence to the rules.

Select an appropriate time and place for confrontations. Neutral turf is usually an important consideration. Be sure you are meeting at a time when the disputants are ready. They should be reasonably rational and cool. Enough time should be allowed to work through emotional issues unhurriedly in a comfortable, distraction-free location. Confrontations are difficult under the best of circumstances. The last thing you need is a ringing telephone or other interruptions.

Determine to what degree there is mutual motivation for dealing with the conflict. If there is no mutual incentive, it is best to delay confrontation until the desire to work things out equalizes. Continually search for and call attention to the benefits each party will receive if the conflict is effectively managed. Unless there is something positive "in it" for all concerned, the situation is likely to continue as is or deteriorate further. Often the disputants are so involved in their own pain that they cannot perceive the payoff for solving the problem. It may be your responsibility to point it out.

Focus energy on points of agreement. If the third party can do nothing else but enable antagonists to begin talking together about something on which they can agree, the most useful conflict-management service will have been performed. The reason why "agreement focus" is so important is that it creates a positive connection between the two parties that did not previously exist. It lets in a ray of hope.

As indicated earlier, time is such a critical factor in conflict management that the faster you can plow through the differences phase (accusations, recriminations, history, antagonisms, ventilation, etc.) and get into the potential areas of agreement, the better the chances for success. Too often individuals and groups

become caught up in arguing about points of entrenched disagreement or in semantic traps that can only intensify anger or
apathy. By working first on what can be agreed on, you build the
success momentum necessary for handling tougher issues later
on.

*Take charge of the communication processes during con-
frontations.* Use your intuition plus the skills and strategies
previously described to control the interactions. For example:

- Do not allow disputants to ramble at length. Without being
  abrasive, suggest getting to the point and intervene whenever necessary to see that each gets equal time.

- Facilitate listening by insisting on restatement or paraphrasing when it is appropriate to be sure each heard the
  other.

- Control interruptions. Restate ground rules as often as
  needed.

- Use paper and pencil. When communication is faltering, ask
  both parties to write their ideas on paper before sharing
  them. The paper-pencil process sometimes assists people in
  thinking more clearly and causes commitment and planning
  to be taken more seriously.

- Encourage role reversal. If the parties are willing, ask
  person A to present his or her side of the issue in no more
  than three minutes *without interruption.* Person B is then
  asked to present person A's perceptions as though he or
  she were person A. The procedure is reversed and both
  parties can then discuss discrepancies in the portrayals.
  This is an old process, but it works effectively. Your job as
  third party is to keep the discussion problem focused and to
  point out similarities and differences that might have been
  missed by the disputants.

Serve as a process observer for the disputants. Every now and
then give them some feedback regarding how they are doing.
Vary this approach from time to time by asking them how they
think they are doing. Get them to focus on the positive features of
their interaction.

Manage the level of tension in the conflict. In some disagreements, the tension level is so low that there is no sense of
urgency and no movement toward getting the problem solved.
The antagonism simply simmers at the aggravation level and
never comes to a head. The third party can help by (1) bringing

disputants face to face, thereby breaking their pattern of selective avoidance; (2) encouraging them to talk about what will happen if they do not work out their differences; and (3) encouraging them to talk about how they feel about each other personally. Conversely, if the tension level is too high, the third party must do more one-on-one work and must carefully structure the confrontations to enhance the climate of emotional safety.

Keep participants in the here and now. The tempting thing to do in conflicts is to dwell on past hurts or predict future catastrophes. The third party can help by continually reiterating, "What are we going to do *now*?"

Build in another third party. If it appears to be an interminable conflict, bring in another person who may have easier access to the disputants. When I used to help students work out their disagreements, I would sometimes ask them to bring in an uninvolved student (whom they both agreed was fair) to serve as a mediator when I was not there. This tactic works equally well with adults.

Continually review for yourself the seven basic steps of mediation.

1. Elicit from one of the disputants a suggestion as to how the problem situation could be handled more effectively.

2. Check out the proposed alternative with the other disputant and obtain a counterproposal if necessary.

3. Continue to elicit and check out suggestions until you arrive at a specific agreement about a course of action.

4. Work out the details of the plan and get commitments to its implementation from both parties. Summarize for each disputant his or her part of the plan.

5. Closely monitor the follow-through and make alternate plans as needed.

6. Do not consider it a failure when people cannot come to an agreement. Look instead at the options available if no agreement is reached.

7. Finally, be persistent and do not give up. Remember, a good psychiatrist always outlasts the patient.

HOW TO HELP GROUPS MANAGE CONFLICT

A few suggestions for working with groups should be mentioned at this point. First of all, if at all possible, avoid becoming mediator between groups. It is a risky and thankless game, particularly if it falls outside the official spheres of negotiation or compulsory arbitration. If, however, you choose to help groups beat their way out of a conflict, let me at least share with you a few lessons that were learned the hard way.

Obtain a clear contract. Be sure all participants know why you are there and what you role is. There is nothing more lethal to successful mediation than imposing a helper or facilitator on a group. It can only ensure hostility.

Take time to answer questions and develop realistic expectations. Let both groups know what will be changing as you work together. Encourage all disputants to challenge your "objectivity," and respond to them without defensiveness.

Persuade the group to give you as much control as possible. The more power the disputants agree to give you, the easier it will be for you to use appropriate interventions and procedural devices to help them manage the conflict.

Allow plenty of time to work. The more people involved, the more time required. Trust is an indispensable condition of conflict management, and it develops very slowly in groups.

Break the group into smaller units as often as possible. Difficulty in helping groups manage conflict increases proportionately with the size of the groups involved. Competence in managing effective communication is probably the most important skill a third party will need. Here are a few tips:

- Use pairs and groups of three or six to mingle people with opposing points of view.

- Assign *specific* tasks to smaller groups so that they will not degenerate into gripe sessions or long, grim silence.

- Never conduct open discussions with the entire group of disputants on hot issues without first having used smaller, less threatening groupings. Spontaneous, town-hall type meetings in conflict climates usually degenerate into opinion-sharing forums or mutual exchanges of ignorance, with little progress toward controlling conflict.

- Ask small groups to report their ideas on paper. Use large sheets of newsprint and felt-tipped markers to maintain an ongoing, easy-to-read record of what has been happening. This process reduces suspicion and tends to open up the dialog. It also avoids long, boring, verbal reports.

Use consensus-seeking techniques when appropriate. Consensus has been described as "getting your say, but not necessarily your way" or "making decisions you can live with but wouldn't die for." Actually it is a process that is often talked about but seldom employed. If used in good faith, however, it can ensure that everyone is at least listened to. The consensus process works best in conflict situations if *all* people involved read the following directions and discuss them thoroughly before implementing them.

Consensus Seeking: How To Get Agreement

1. Avoid arguing for your own individual judgment. Present your position as clearly as possible but listen to other members' reactions and consider their positions before pressing your point.

2. Do not assume that someone must win and someone must lose when discussion reaches a stalemate. Instead, look for the next most acceptable alternative for all. Keep the discussion focused on what you can agree on, even if it is only one small point.

3. Do not change your mind simply to avoid conflict. Be suspicious when agreement comes too quickly and easily, because this may mean acquiescence and not acceptance. Acquiescence means going along but not really agreeing. Acceptance means true agreement and commitment to follow through.

4. Avoid conflict-resolving techniques such as majority vote, averaging, coin flips, and bargaining. When a dissenting member finally agrees, do not feel that he or she must be rewarded later.

5. Differences of opinion are natural and they are to be expected. Disagreements can help the group decide, because a wide range of information provides a greater chance for the group to find more effective solutions.

6. When you cannot get anywhere in a large group, break into smaller groups and try to reach consensus. Then return to the larger group and try again.

7. When one or two members simply cannot agree with the group after a reasonable period of time, ask them to deliver a minority report stating their positions.

Try these two strategies for handling conflict in groups:

Strategy 1. (Use when personal animosities prevent dealing with substantive issues.)

- Both groups are brought together and divided into smaller groups of six to eight, with each group containing equal representation of opposing points of view. The groups are asked to discuss their basic points of disagreement for *no longer than ten minutes.*

- The two opposing groups are then physically separated (sent to different rooms if possible) and each is asked to list on newsprint what the other group does that is causing disagreement. This question may be asked: "What does the other group do that irritates you or that causes you problems?" The groups should focus on basic disagreements or resentments.

- After completing the first list, each group is asked to list on another sheet what the members imagine the *other* group is writing about *them.*

- The two groups are brought together. The newsprint charts are posted and read without any formal report. The groups are then asked, "What do you think about this? Any surprises? Is there anything you can agree on?" They should attempt to identify similarities of perception and points of possible agreement.

- Discussion may then continue. The basic communication techniques previously described can be used.

Strategy 2. (Use to clarify the positions of large numbers of people on a particular point of contention.)

- At any appropriate point during a discussion of differences, a values continuum may be drawn on newsprint or chalkboard with opposing points of view at each end, as indicated by the following drawing.

Implementing the new flexible-time schedule

Totally Against	Acceptable with Modifications	Totally For

Controlling smoking in the office

Against	Acceptable Under Certain Conditions	For

- Each group member places a mark on the line to represent his or her position. Often people on different sides of the same issue are not as far apart as they thought they were. In fact, they often bunch up in the center. This activity has the advantage of depicting in a graphic way group perceptions regarding a particular conflict.

- A variation of this strategy can also be effective. A line (imaginary or real) is drawn on the floor from wall to wall, and the two walls are designated as positive and negative. Then the members are asked to *stand* along this continuum according to the intensity of their feelings about a given issue.

Avoid intimidating yourself. Third parties often become scapegoats and targets for frustrated adversaries. If you are attacked, remind the antagonists that *they* asked *you* to help them with their mess. Then remind yourself that such displaced antagonism is a natural part of the process and will usually stop rather quickly when confronted directly.

If everything fails, end the relationship. If you feel that what is going on is nonproductive, confront the group with your perception, and say that you feel it necessary to end your participation. It is more than likely you will be asked to continue. You will then have re-established your purpose *and* your power. Sometimes a *terminal* intervention will help both groups realize that they have been spinning their wheels and that it is time to get back on the track and work out some solutions.

COMMENT

Study this chapter carefully and consider all the pitfalls before agreeing to be a mediator. To mediate a disagreement between two of your best friends may mean the loss of both friendships. The success of third-party interventions depends on the knowledge and skill of the intervener, the good will of the disputants, and countless other situational factors. Sometimes third parties serve no purpose but to surface issues so value laden and so aggravated that they are beyond mediation. In such cases, assistance can still be given to help disputants learn to live with their pain. This happens quite often when marriage counseling does not work out and it becomes divorce counseling, thus assisting the husband and wife to cope the best they can with their separation. Although this may not seem like a happy ending, it does manage the conflict in a way that might not have been possible without third-party help.

Chapter 7

What To Do When You Lose

If at first you don't succeed, try, try, again. Then quit. There's no sense being a damn fool about it.

W.C. Fields

Sooner or later you will encounter a conflict that is not only unavoidable and unmanageable, but that also threatens your self-esteem. It will be an impasse in which you may perceive yourself as—do I dare use the word?—a *loser.* Feeling like a loser in this win-at-all-costs society is hard to bear, partly because we have been persuaded by countless television commercials that it is not nice to lose and if we do lose, there must be something wrong with us. The acceptable national norm of winning is reinforced daily by the pervasive power of advertising as it impacts all areas of our lives.[26] Nevertheless, the law of averages virtually guarantees an occasional interpersonal "defeat" that—in spite of our best efforts—can cause us to feel used, victimized, or helpless.

Think about what your feelings or behaviors might be in any of the following conflict situations.

- A colleague refuses to stop smoking in your commonly shared work area. Despite countless confrontations and appeals, there is no change.

- You have exhausted all your resources in trying to persuade one of your suppliers to replace a faulty product. You are stuck with it.

- Your liability insurance rates rise astronomically following a minor accident. After numerous contacts up and down the management ladder, the final word is "Take it or leave it; those are your new rates."

---

[26]For more about the power of television and the psychology of self-esteem, see Glasser (1972).

- Your neighbor continually plays loud music late at night despite your repeated requests, threats, and pleas. You have done everything you can, and there is no change.
- You are more competent than the last few employees who were promoted while you were by-passed. You know this and it has been validated by your supervisor, but you are at a dead end because of the company's affirmative-action promotion policy.
- You lose an argument with a maitre d' about unacknowledged reservations that you made a week in advance. There you are, with an important client and no other suitable restaurants in the area.
- You are blamed by your supervisor for something you did not do. Your endless explanations do no good.
- You are in chronic conflict with an alcoholic co-worker who is also your close friend. He refuses all help as the destructive and dangerous behavior continues.
- Perhaps you already have an unresolvable conflict.

  Describe it here: _____

  _____

  _____

  _____

  _____

THE CONFLICT-DISTRESS CYCLE

Such examples could continue interminably since we all live with unique collections of conflicts that will not go away: conflicts that have the potential for causing serious stress-related diseases. And each time we are involved in intense or prolonged situations such as the ones described above, a cycle of involuntary psycho-physiological reactions begins. A certain amount of stress is helpful in keeping us alert, functional, and motivated. The conflict-distress cycle, however, refers to what Selye (1974) calls "distress," i.e., the kind of excessive stress that disrupts physical, mental, and emotional equilibrium and makes one sick. This cycle accelerates the aging process and can cause serious damage to our bodies. The following paragraphs explain the cycle,[27] and it is illustrated in Figure 7.

External conflict stressors, such as unyielding insurance companies, uncooperative neighbors or co-workers, intransigent manufacturers and bureaucrats, a stubborn spouse, or an alcoholic family member,

usually cause you to

talk to yourself in desperate, negative ways—such as "I'll never be able to live with this." "If only I had . . . " or "I'll show them!" and to continue this type of self-talk long after the incident has passed. This negative self-talk

then causes your brain to

trigger the secretion of hormones that mobilize your body to deal with danger. Since the part of your brain that secretes these hormones does not think, it does not determine whether you are being attacked by a rabid dog or aggravated by a troublesome thought. It only perceives *trouble;* therefore, you receive the same internal chemical bath

that causes

elevated blood pressure, faster heartbeat, interrupted digestion, tense muscles, and other conditions that prepare you to fight physically or to run away. Since it is usually not socially acceptable to do either,

we usually

engage in unproductive behavior, such as grimly eating our anger and getting an upset stomach or a heart attack, losing our tempers and making fools of ourselves, or remaining in a chronically irritable condition. Such behaviors cause more negative self-talk as we punish ourselves for our stupid behavior. This negative self-talk

again causes the brain

to precipitate the secretion of the same fight-or-flight hormones in response to our increasing tension. Thus the distress cycle continues, sometimes even causing us to start this unproductive cycle in others.

[27]This is a simplified description of the way in which the brain affects the body in stressful situations and of how the brain essentially works against itself. For further information, read Selye (1974).

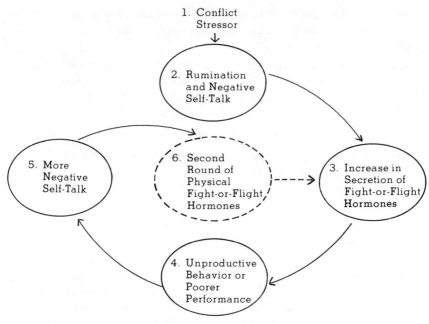

Figure 7. The Conflict-Distress Cycle

FOUR SYSTEMS OF PERSONAL NURTURE

To avoid stress-related illnesses, we must learn how to take intelligent care of ourselves, especially during those times when our usual conflict-coping resources seem inadequate. When you feel the stress cycle beginning, break it by using one or more of the following systems of personal nurture.

System 1: Physical Activity

Within the limits of your physical capacity (which can best be determined in consultation with your physician) spend *at least* fifteen minutes on sustained exercise that raises your heart rate over one hundred beats per minute. Short bursts of exercise such as punching a bag or running up a flight of stairs may temporarily relieve tension, but it will not produce the benefits of longer periods of aerobic exercise [28] and may even prove dangerous by making sudden and overtaxing demands on an unprepared or poorly conditioned body.

[28]*Aerobic exercise* is defined as "sustained oxygen-producing exercise" and is described in detail by Cooper (1970).

The two basic advantages of aerobic exercise are the following:

1. After about thirty minutes of fairly strenuous exercise, the body releases antidepressive chemicals that promote feelings of well-being and in some cases euphoria. More and more experts in exercise physiology are concurring in the opinion that it is almost impossible to be depressed after a period of sustained heavy exercise.

2. Regular noncompetitive exercise has enormous potential for increasing confidence and feelings of self-worth—both of which are beneficial in mitigating the impact of losing. In his study of people who had become "positively addicted" to exercise, Glasser (1976) notes:

> People describe mental alertness, increased self-awareness, a physical feeling of well-being. Over and over again people report a *sense of confidence,* perhaps the single most often used words to describe the benefits of their addiction. Many describe that they are more tolerant and less angry. (p. 98)

The form of sustained exercise that you select must be pleasant and easy to do. It has to fit your life style or it will not work. The discipline needed to become a serious runner, swimmer, or cyclist is too difficult for most people to develop and the attrition rate of those who embark on overly ambitious exercise programs is high. The most available form of aerobic exercise is fast walking—about four miles per hour or about sixty-five steps per minute. (Count one step each time your left foot touches the ground). Walking off your stress is possible almost anywhere, but regardless of the exercise you select, it is important to internalize the idea that physical activity has high payoff in reducing the injurious effects of unresolved conflict.

System 2: Thought Control

Since our noisy, worrying, ruminating cerebral cortex places us in the stress cycle, why not use that same part of our brain to help break out of it? By talking more rationally to ourselves we can reduce the stress of painful conflicts. Several approaches may be used in addition to those described in Chapter 4. Consider using any or all of the following:

1. *Positive Denial.* The process of temporarily denying that something bad is happening is not always destructive. According to Richard Lazarus in an interview by Goleman (1979), denial can often buy the time needed to adjust to a difficult situation as long

as the denial does not result in unhealthy distortion of reality. Lazarus suggests:[29]

> Life is ambiguous. Many of the beliefs we have about the world around us—about justice, about our integrity, about the attitudes of those around us, about our own future—are based on, at best, ambiguous information. One can maintain illusions about those that have a positive aura without necessarily distorting reality. Such illusions are not pathological; hope is not the same as denial. (p. 45)

Examples of short-term positive denial are found all around us: the newly divorced person, the patient who has his or her worst fears confirmed by the medical lab, or the person experiencing the unexpected loss of a loved one. In many such cases, initial denial of the painful reality cushions the shock until the requisite emotional strength and support have been gathered.

The practice of positive denial, when applied to seemingly unmanageable conflicts, at least allows us to capitalize on the positive power of hope.

2. Healthy Distraction. Look for ways of distracting yourself from uncontrollable conflicts by keeping busy. Schedule activities that require attention and concentration. Games, puzzles, writing letters, construction, playing musical instruments, cooking, reading, and countless other activities can be combined with thought stopping to avoid stress-related worry. It helps to keep a list handy of things that you really enjoy doing and that require concentration. When you are under stress, this list can remind you to put your thoughts in another place.

Use your sixth sense—your sense of humor—as an avenue to healthy personal distraction. By focusing on the absurdity of some conflict events, humor provides momentary escape from shattering situations and sometimes decreases your perception of their importance.

3. Altered Perception. How conflict situations are perceived in our minds determines the emotions that are triggered. When what is actually happening does not match what we *believe should be happening,* we usually get upset.

It is difficult but possible to lower our stress level in no-win situations by suspending judgment, distancing ourselves mentally from the conflict, and simply altering our perceptions by concentrating on the minute details of the moment. For example, if

[29]Reprinted from: D. Goleman. Positive Denial: The Case for Not Facing Reality. *Psychology Today* Magazine, November 1979. Copyright © 1979, Ziff Davis Publishing Co. Used with permission.

you are involved in what appears to be a hopeless conflict with a TV repairman who refuses to do anything about his shoddy work, try shutting down your judging mechanism, which is bombarding you with messages about how unfair he is, and focus instead on what is actually happening and what you can realistically plan to do about it. Move from Self-talk 1 to Self-talk 2.

- Self-talk 1 (valuing, judging, or criticizing): "This turkey thinks he can get away with ripping me off. They are all alike and I'll be damned if I'm going to get taken again."
- Self-talk 2 (observing or describing): "My television set still doesn't work. This person refuses to fix it even though he's been paid. We seem to be standing here shouting at each other. So far he has not changed his mind. What are my options?"

By altering our perception of what is happening, the possibilities of setting up the stress cycle are markedly reduced. The technique of lowering our perceptual order under pressure is not easy, but it can be practiced daily in minor conflicts until it is mastered. The skill on which to concentrate is learning to talk to yourself in terms of *observing and describing* events rather than *judging and criticizing* them.

4. *Acceptance, not Toleration.* When faced with the stress of a conflict that we cannot change, we can talk to ourselves about it in three basic ways:

- Acceptance: "I've made my peace with it. I will sublimate my desires and learn to be more satisfied with less in this situation."
- Nonacceptance: "I'm going to beat this thing. I'll struggle against it until I win, escape, change, or die."
- Tolerance: "I'll put up with it but I'll resent every minute."

Numbers one and two are probably better for your health in the long run. Nonacceptance at least keeps your energy mobilized. Acceptance implies seeking out ways in which to work with yourself in handling an unpleasantness. Both acceptance and nonacceptance are more proactive, honest, and hopeful coping processes than is resentful tolerance, which invariably turns into self-destructive anger.

5. *Reprograming Our Belief Systems.* Many no-win conflicts are aggravated by certain irrational beliefs that were programed into our brains at a very early age. Beliefs such as "Certain acts are wrong or wicked, and people who perform them should be punished " or "We must be loved by everyone, and everyone must approve of everything we do " may continue to influence how we react to the behavior of others throughout our lives. By getting in touch with these irrational beliefs and consciously disputing them in our minds, our vulnerability to the stress of conflict should diminish.[30] Three helpful questions which people can ask when they become aware of being angry, hurt, frustrated, or entangled in an irrational belief are:

- What am I feeling?
- What am I reacting to?
- What am I doing to keep myself feeling this way?

These questions focus on personal responsibility for feelings and introduce a cognitive element into one's response to a conflict. The process in itself represents the return to a more functional level of behavior.

6. *Cultivating Patience.* Patience is an anodyne for the pain of losing. Perceiving time as an agent of healing rather than as a period of suffering is a more productive and useful way to think. Patience is nothing more than creative waiting. It is possible to convince both your conscious and your unconscious mind that things will get better by continually repeating to yourself in high stress situations (whether you believe them or not) platitudes such as:

- "One day at a time."
- "Tomorrow I'll feel better."
- "This too shall pass."
- "Nothing lasts forever."
- The A.A. prayer (see Chapter 3).
- Your own favorite platitude: _____

_____

7. *Learning from Mistakes.* Whenever you experience pain or do something stupid that you cannot undo, ask yourself, "What can I learn from this that will keep me from feeling this miserable again?" By looking for valuable lessons, we may learn to overcome

---

[30]More information on reprograming our belief systems can be found in Ellis and Harper (1976).

a weakness or find an unknown source of support. Such dis-coveries or insights can change our focus from pain to growth and can markedly enhance our sense of personal power. This does not mean that all losing conflicts are good for us or that they "build character," but there may be a way to salvage something positive out of any unpleasantness.

8. Writing Things Down. When you are really down after being on the losing end of a win-lose conflict, write down your feelings and whatever else comes into your mind. Keep some writing tablets handy and record elaborate lists of what you would like to do to your number-one adversary. Make plans, throw insults, consider options, and write them all on paper. Then read it over once or twice and put it away. Doing this a few times may motivate you to keep a journal to help clarify your perception of yourself.[31]

No one seems to know exactly why writing things down tends to relieve anxiety, but it apparently works for many people. Perhaps a different perspective is developed after observing one's honest thoughts in black and white. Perhaps the act of writing itself is a stress reducer.

System 3: Letting Go

Letting go of the negative rumination and stress-producing emotions that accompany nonproductive conflicts requires sepa-rating the thinking part of the brain, which deals with the external world, from the nonthinking part, which controls our internal biochemical processes. This is not an easy thing to do. Whereas System 2 is directed at reprograming our self-talk, System 3 attempts to *shut down* the self-talk and allow the mind to rest.

Meditation, in its broadest definition, is the most commonly accepted way of letting go of our internal chatter, but there are well over a hundred methods. Select one that seems good for you and that fits your temperament and life style. You could start with the process recommended by Benson and Klipper (1975), who have synthesized many elements of relaxation and meditation into what they call the relaxation response:[32]

---

[31]For more about the value of writing and personal journals consult Simons (1978).

[32]Reprinted from: *The Relaxation Response* by Herbert Benson, M.D., with Miriam Z. Klipper. Copyright © 1975 by William Morrow and Company, Inc. By permission of the publisher.

(1) Sit quietly in a comfortable position.

(2) Close your eyes.

(3) Deeply relax all your muscles, beginning at your feet and progressing up to your face. Keep them relaxed.

(4) Breathe through your nose. Become aware of your breathing. As you breathe out, say the word, "ONE," silently to yourself. For example, breathe IN . . . OUT, "ONE"; IN . . . OUT, "ONE"; etc. Breathe easily and naturally.

(5) Continue for 10 to 20 minutes. You may open your eyes to check the time, but do not use an alarm. When you finish, sit quietly for several minutes, at first with your eyes closed and later with your eyes opened. Do not stand up for a few minutes.

(6) Do not worry about whether you are successful in achieving a deep level of relaxation. Maintain a passive attitude and permit relaxation to occur at its own pace. When distracting thoughts occur, try to ignore them by not dwelling upon them and return to repeating "ONE." With practice, the response should come with little effort. Practice the technique once or twice daily, but not within two hours after any meal, since the digestive processes seem to interfere with the elicitation of the Relaxation Response. (pp. 114-115)

The key to this method of letting go is the repetition of the word "one." Keeping the thinking part of your brain occupied, concentrating on the repetition, prevents it from driving your nonthinking midbrain crazy with internal dialog. For a few minutes your body returns to a balanced and serene state.

If the relaxation response does not work for you, there are plenty of others that might. LeShan (1974) describes many systems of meditation and provides some helpful admonitions for the reader.

Guided imagery has recently been found to have some positive effect in the treatment of some catastrophic illnesses. The power of the process is that it enables us to communicate with our unconscious minds in ways previously not attempted. There is evidence to indicate that our unconscious often does not respond to logic or to words, but instead to mental pictures or images. Learning ways of relaxing and visualizing improved conditions will often enable us to reduce the pain of frustrating conflicts.[33]

---

[33]For more on this subject, read Simonton, Simonton, and Creighton (1978) and Lande (1979).

System 4: Social and Environmental Nurturing

The pain of living with the fallout of a stressful no-win conflict can often be mitigated by manipulating our physical surroundings and/or social relationships. Some ways to do this follow:

1. Distancing. Even if you are unable to completely escape from your conflict stressor, work on some ways of decreasing the toxic time spent with that person. Terminate distressing phone calls assertively. Practice and use distraction techniques (described in Chapter 4) to psychologically get away from the situation. Physically walk away from an unpleasant encounter without feeling guilty. Practice moving away from nonproductive encounters with as much grace as possible. For more ideas about how to terminate toxic relationships read Greenwald (1973) and M.J. Smith (1975).

2. Aesthetics. Beauty in any form has a soothing influence on the jangled spirit. Use it to break the conflict-stress cycle by increasing your contact with pleasant sights and sounds. When your interpersonal world is deteriorating, take a beauty break. Get some space around you that pleases your eye: a large body of water, mountains, a forest, a golf course, or whatever nourishes your mood. Listen to some pleasant and relaxing music. Study a painting or read something inspirational. Moving toward beauty and away from interpersonal ugliness can be a life-enhancing (and life-prolonging) practice.

3. Diversification. The more interests, activities, and positive relationships that you maintain, the less vulnerable you are likely to be when faced with the inevitable lose-lose conflict. A constricted life style, on the other hand, tends to keep us dependent on one or two sources of personal validation; when things go bad in those areas of our lives, it usually means more intense distress, because all of our emotional eggs are in one basket. A broad choice of people to relate to and a wide range of activities with which to occupy oneself productively are probably the most powerful antidotes to the temporary pain of no-win conflict.

4. Support Systems. One of the most effective ways to reduce the stress of conflict is to establish a powerful network of interpersonal support. Research from almost everywhere indicates that a lack of satisfying human relationships can lead to ill health. Most of us need significant others to turn to when we feel isolated, anxious, threatened, or insecure, yet such relationships are becoming increasingly scarce. In our complicated world, a broad base of support is important to our emotional and even our physical survival. In addition to friends and family to nurture us, we need others to respect us, challenge us, and serve as role models, mentors, evaluators, or energizers.

A good support system leaves one feeling stronger and better able to draw on his or her own resources. The following list illustrates some possible functions of support systems and how they can be used to reduce conflict-related stress.

- *Role Models:* Observe a few people who can help define courses of action and who have keen insights on how to handle destructive conflict.

- *Those Who Share Common Interests:* Those who share our common interests can be especially valuable in helping us with healthy distraction. These are associates with whom we can bowl, visit museums, play tennis or bridge, share ideas, go to movies, or otherwise get a respite from our problems.

- *Close Friends:* Friends can help provide nurturance and keep us from becoming isolated and alienated. Add to this category people who have known you for a long time, who respect your competence, and who can provide, when needed, the support necessary to bolster your sagging self-esteem.

- *Helpers:* Some people can be depended on in a crisis to provide assistance. These supporters may have expertise in assisting with particular kinds of problems and may not be the type with whom one would choose to have a close personal relationship.

- *Referral Agents:* These people can put you in touch with special resources through their knowledge of people and organizations.

- *Challengers:* These may question the inadequate way you are handling a given conflict. Although challengers may at times be abrasive and demanding, they may be just what you need to climb out of a rut or to develop the motivation to try some new behaviors.

Because it is unlikely that you will find all these qualities in one person, it is important to seek out, nurture, and maintain various valuable support systems. Keeping a support system up to date requires an ongoing assessment of available resources as one's life changes. Work at staying in contact with the people whom you value; they are better than medical or life insurance.

COMMENT

The hardest fact to face about interpersonal conflict is that you will probably lose at least as often as you win, yet there is no need to jeopardize your health by succumbing to the dangerous cycle of conflict-related stress. You are not powerless. These four systems for weathering these inevitable low points in your life are just the beginning. The rest is up to you. The final chapter of this book will give you many additional resources for specific areas in your quest for ways to manage conflict from the inside out.

Chapter 8

How To Learn More
About Conflict Management

*Personally I am always ready to learn,
although I do not always like being taught.*

Sir Winston Churchill

While searching for practical and teachable ways to handle
conflict, I found certain publications to be especially useful. The
following annotated references not only provide information and
insight, but also motivate the reader to keep seeking or inventing
newer and better conflict-management strategies as situations
change. I continue to recommend these publications in workshops,
lectures, and personal-skill-building seminars. They are briefly
described on the following pages in hopes that they may provide
stimulation without exerting too much influence, because no
single philosophy or system, no matter how appealing, should be
swallowed whole. Following the annotated references is a list of
the other works that are cited throughout this book.

Alberti, R.E., & Emmons, M.L. *Your perfect right.* San Luis Obispo, CA:
Impact Press, 1970.

This is perhaps the first significant popular book written about
assertiveness training. *Your Perfect Right* is semitechnical but easy
to read. The authors use a solid research base to explain the differences among assertive, nonassertive, and aggressive behavior.
The book provides a basic grounding in assertiveness theory and
includes practice exercises in specific techniques that will add to
your skill in handling conflict.

Arnold, J.D. *Make up your mind.* New York: AMACOM, 1978.

When you arrive at the point in a conflict that requires problem
solving, John Arnold's book can help with the details. The seven
building blocks of individual or cooperative decision making help
balance logic against emotions and smoke out the real issues. In the
glossary is a check list of criteria for making effective personal and

professional decisions. Admittedly a "systems" problem-solving book, it is nonetheless helpful.

Bach, G.R., & Goldberg, H. *Creative aggression.* New York: Avon Books, 1974.

A powerful message points out the dangers of being too "nice." This is a basic assertion-training manual designed to show the reader how to productively use anger and other natural emotions. Bach and Goldberg expose the veneer of sweetness and light that mask much illness-producing hostility. They make specific suggestions about how to confront conflict in healthier and more effective ways.

Benson, H., & Klipper, M.Z. *The relaxation response.* New York: William Morrow, 1975.

This book describes the simplest of all meditative techniques and supports its value with strong medical evidence. By going through a six-step routine it is possible to achieve complete mental and physical relaxation. The potential for revitalization is obvious, as is its utility in providing relief from the tension of conflict.

Bolton, R. *People skills.* Englewood Cliffs, NJ: Prentice-Hall, 1979.

This communication-skills handbook provides detailed help in eliminating the roadblocks that cause and aggravate conflict. Chapters 12 and 13 relate specifically to the prevention and control of conflict and to handling the emotional components of conflict. Both the student of human behavior and the layman will find Bolton's book a rich source of conflict-management information.

Davis, M., Eshelman, E., & McKay, M. *The relaxation and stress reduction workbook.* Richmond, CA: New Harbinger, 1980.

This practical workbook goes into detail about how to employ specific stress-reduction techniques, such as: progressive relaxation, self-hypnosis, meditation, autogenics, imagination, refuting irrational ideas, assertiveness training, biofeedback, breathing, time management, and thought stopping. Procedures are described in easy-to-read, planning-and-practice units, well designed for maximum utility.

Ellis, A., & Harper, R.A. *A new guide to rational living.* North Hollywood, CA: Wilshire, 1976.

The authors present a system of understanding and controlling one's thinking that is useful in conflict situations. Based on Ellis' well-known psychology of Rational Emotive Therapy (you feel the way you think), specific suggestions and examples are presented to enable people to accept the world and to develop a powerful system of honest self-analysis. By learning and practicing this system, it is possible to confront conflicts with greater confidence and to accept losses with greater equanimity. A few of the more provocative chapter titles are "How You Create Your Feelings," "How to Stop

Blaming and Start Living," "Living Rationally in an Irrational World," and "Does Reason Always Prove Reasonable?"

Friedman, M., & Rosenman, R.H. *Type A behavior and your heart.* Greenwich, CT: Fawcett Books, 1978.

According to Friedman and Rosenman, two eminent cardiologists, persistent conflict and stress may be the result of Type-A (hard-driving, competitive, and hurried) behavior. The medical information in this easy-to-read book interested me less than did the stop-and-smell-the-flowers philosophy proposed by the authors as an antidote to the conflict-prone personality. Specific exercises are suggested to achieve a life-style change that may prevent heart disease.

Glasser, W. *The identity society.* New York: Harper & Row, 1972.

Glasser clearly explains the gradual shift since 1940 from a goal-oriented (survival) society to a role-oriented (identity) society. Rights, affluence, and the media—especially television—have, according to the author, produced a cultural gap of much greater significance than the generation gap. Chapter Six discusses reality therapy as a system of helping people in conflict deal more effectively with their lives.

Gordon, T. *Parent effectiveness training.* New York: Wyden, 1970.

Gordon, T. *Teacher effectiveness training.* New York: Wyden, 1974.

Gordon, T. *Leader effectiveness training.* New York: Wyden, 1977.

All three books carry the same solid interpersonal-relations messages adapted for different audiences. The first message addresses the question of how to determine "who owns the problem" in a conflict situation. The second describes how to communicate clearly and assertively by learning to send "I" messages, and Gordon's third message deals with how to listen "actively" (for feelings as well as content). Specific exercises related to these recurring themes may be useful in the identification and management of conflict.

Greenwald, J. *Be the person you were meant to be.* New York: Dell, 1973.

Interpersonal conflict, according to Greenwald, is the result of toxic relationships. This book tells how to recognize toxic behavior in yourself and in others and how to develop a more emotionally nourishing life style. Greenwald's use of Gestalt principles and his heavy emphasis on self-knowledge (the key to conflict management) can provide a rich insight into one's self-limiting behaviors. You may recognize yourself and others in many of the examples described in Chapter 7, "Antidotes to Toxic Relating."

Herman, S.M., & Korenich, M. *Authentic management: A Gestalt orientation to organizations and their development.* Reading, MA: Addison-Wesley, 1977.

This powerful little book is filled with useful, common-sense ideas about human behavior in organizations. In a playful yet clear and convincing style, the authors suggest ways to confront conflict. The exercises found in Section Four have been particularly helpful to me in assisting clients to discover their own styles and to use them to deal in the "here and now" with specific situations.

James, M., & Jongeward, D. *Born to win.* Reading, MA: Addison-Wesley, 1975.

This easy-to-understand manual of workable transactional analysis ("I'm O.K.; You're O.K.") is combined with Gestalt ("here and now") awareness exercises. The theory and activities promote the kind of insight that is indispensable in managing intrapersonal or interpersonal conflict. By clearly presenting information about crossed (conflictive) transactions, stroke hunger, life scripts, and other transactional-analysis concepts, the authors lead the reader toward an awareness of the kinds of insight and interpersonal skills needed in dealing with our contentious times.

Kelley, C. *Assertion training: A facilitator's guide.* San Diego, CA: University Associates, 1979.

This training guide synthesizes the best current assertion-training techniques and provides a number of activities that can be used by groups or individuals to learn to recognize and practice assertive behavior.

Lakein, A. *How to get control of your time and your life.* New York: Signet Books, 1974.

Effective time management is closely related to conflict management. When your priorities are well established and you understand your preferences and your bottom lines, many anxieties dissipate as life becomes less contentious. Lakein approaches time management from a whole-life perspective that assists readers in developing plans and purposes without becoming compulsive. The book is sensible and does not create in the reader the sense of guilt that one so often feels when studying time management.

LeShan, L. *How to meditate: A guide to self-discovery.* Boston, MA: Little, Brown, 1974.

LeShan, a respected pioneer in altered-consciousness training, has broad experience as a researcher, psychotherapist, and teacher. He has for many years explored the utilitarian aspects of meditation in a scientific and sensible way. This little book can help the reader develop some personal criteria for evaluating conflict-reducing meditative and relaxation techniques and avoid the wasted time and disappointment that often accompany the quick-and-easy systems that overpromise and underdeliver.

Powell, J. *Why am I afraid to tell you who I am?* Niles, IL: Argus, 1969.

In addition to building awareness and insight into the reasons why we all seem to hide our true selves from each other, this little book helps readers in two specific ways: (1) understanding and improving communication with those closest to them and (2) making the most productive use of conflict when it inevitably occurs. This is a good book to read with a significant other. Powell explains all of this with the eloquent simplicity that characterizes his writing.

Schur, E. *The awareness trap: Self-absorption instead of social change.* New York: McGraw-Hill, 1977.

Schur deals with the fascinating concept of self-absorption run rampant—a refreshing change from the glib promises, buzz words, and reality evasions produced by the self-awareness craze of the seventies. Incorporating some of Schur's mature and responsible ideas in our daily efforts to handle interpersonal and social disputes may result in lasting and realistic benefits.

Selye, H., M.D. *Stress without distress.* New York: Lippincott, 1974.

This excellent primer about stress is written by the world's leading authority on the topic. Selye presents a reasonable and useful combination of physiology and philosophy that gives the reader some ideas about leading a balanced and productive life. The value of this book in the study of conflict management is in its suggestions about how to achieve optimally productive levels of stress and how to avoid the type of stress that is physically harmful.

Simon, S. *Negative criticism.* Niles, IL: Argus, 1978.

This useful book re-emphasizes the futility of negative criticism. Simon describes with a light touch some specific strategies for taking care of yourself without damaging others when you are the target of criticism.

Simon, S., Howe, L., & Kirschenbaum, H. *Values clarification.* New York: Hart, 1972.

The most difficult conflicts to manage are based on personal value and belief systems. *Values Clarification* is one of the first books—and probably the most significant—on this topic. By reading the short introduction and reviewing some of the exercises, one can quickly gain an appreciation of the power of values clarification as a tool for managing conflict more effectively.

Smith, M.J. *When I say no, I feel guilty.* New York: Dial, 1975.

This is a "how-to" assertiveness training guide in which the author walks the reader through a variety of assertion processes, among which are "broken record" (calm repetition of what you want), "fogging" (acceptance of manipulative criticism by acknowledgement while allowing yourself to remain the judge of what you do), "negative assertion" (acceptance of your faults without having to apologize), and "workable compromise" (protection of your self-respect in bargaining or compromising). The dialogs and examples assist the reader in selecting the skills that are applicable to the conflicts in their own lives.

Toffler, A. *Future shock.* New York: Bantam, 1971.

A thorough reading of *Future Shock* is a valuable education in the causes of many disruptions in our lives. An understanding of the social upheaval of the times may help develop an awareness of the personal options one has in dealing with the accompanying interpersonal conflicts.

Toffler, A. *The third wave.* New York: William Morrow, 1980.

By the author of *Future Shock,* this book gives additional insights.

Walton, R.E. *Interpersonal peacemaking.* Reading, MA: Addison-Wesley, 1969.

This book provides helpful techniques for effectively confronting and working out conflicts in an organizational environment. Walton deals with conflict management "basics" such as mutual motivation, power, balance, open dialog, and optimum tension levels. Various interpersonal examples and scenarios are used to illustrate the author's points. Many of the ideas can be transferred to nonorganizational settings.

University Associates, Inc., 8517 Production Avenue, P.O. Box 26240, San Diego, California 92126.

This organization makes available a remarkably comprehensive assortment of up-to-date and practical behavioral-science materials. Their *Annual Handbook for Group Facilitators* (which has been published yearly since 1972) is a particularly rich source of information. The following selected references from the *Handbooks* are annotated as examples of the type of material that might be useful to those interested in learning more about handling conflict.

Hanson, P.C. The Johari window: A model for soliciting and giving feedback. In J.E. Jones & J.W. Pfeiffer (Eds.), *The 1973 annual handbook for group facilitators.* San Diego, CA: University Associates, 1973.

The author deals with the Johari window as a self-study model through which one can become more aware of conditions that interfere with effective interpersonal communication.

Jones, J.E., & Banet, A.G., Jr. Dealing with anger. In J.W. Pfeiffer & J.E. Jones (Eds.), *The 1976 annual handbook for group facilitators.* San Diego, CA: University Associates, 1976.

This full, concise exploration of the anger cycle shows how this powerful emotion is triggered by threat. Suggestions for dealing with personal anger and with the anger of others are included.

Pfeiffer, J.W., & Jones, J.E. Openness, collusion and feedback. In J.W. Pfeiffer & J.E. Jones (Eds.), *The 1972 annual handbook for group facilitators.* San Diego, CA: University Associates, 1972.

The authors discuss the problems of openness as they are experienced in human communication and explore the concept of "strategic openness" as a satisfying and effective mode of relating to others.

Stepsis, J.A. Conflict-resolution strategies. In J.W. Pfeiffer & J.E. Jones (Eds.), *The 1974 annual handbook for group facilitators.* San Diego, CA: University Associates, 1974.

This is a short, helpful essay on the avoidance, defusion, and confrontation strategies for dealing with conflict plus suggestions for more effective negotiation.

ADDITIONAL REFERENCES

Ardell, D.B. *High level wellness.* Emmaus, PA: Rodale, 1977.

Bliss, E.C. *Getting things done.* New York: Charles Scribner's Sons, 1976.

Bombeck, E. *Aunt Erma's cope book: How to get from Monday to Friday in 12 days.* New York: McGraw-Hill, 1979.

Bronfenbrenner, U. Crime and vandalism permeate nation's schools. *NEA Reporter,* February 1976.

Browne, H. *How I found freedom in an unfree world.* New York: Avon, 1975.

Coles, R. *What about moral sensibility?* Address to the NEA National Accountability Conference, Washington, D.C., March 1981.

Cooper, K. *Aerobics.* New York: M. Evans, 1970.

Cousins, N. *Anatomy of an illness as perceived by the patient.* New York: Norton Press, 1979.

Dreikurs, R. *Psychology in the classroom.* New York: Harper & Row, 1957.

Drucker, P. *Management.* New York: Harper & Row, 1973.

Dubos, R. *Saturday Review,* December 14, 1974.

Frankl, V. *Man's search for meaning.* New York: Simon & Schuster, 1959.

Glasser, W. *Positive addiction.* New York: Harper & Row, 1976.

Goleman, D. Positive denial: The case for not facing reality. *Psychology Today,* November 1979, pp. 44-60.

Hatfield, E., & Walster, G.W. *A new look at love.* Reading, MA: Addison-Wesley, 1978.

Jacobsen, E. *You must relax.* New York: McGraw-Hill, 1978.

Karras, C. *The negotiating game.* New York: Crowell, 1970.

Karras, C. *Give and take.* New York: Crowell, 1974.

Keyes, K. *Handbook to higher consciousness.* St. Mary, KY: Living Love Center, 1973.

Kirschenbaum, H. *Advanced value clarification.* San Diego, CA: University Associates, 1977.

Korda, M. *Power: How to get it and how to use it.* New York: Random House, 1975.

Lande, N. *Mindstyles, lifestyles.* Los Angeles: Price, Stern, Sloan, 1976.

Lande, N. *The emotional maintenance manual.* New York: Rawson, Wade, 1979.

Leonard, G. *The silent pulse.* New York: Dutton, 1978.

McCamy, J.C., & Presley, J. *Human life styling.* New York: Harper & Row, 1975.

Nierenberg, G.I. *The art of negotiating.* New York: Cornerstone Library, 1968.

Porter, E.H. *Strength deployment inventory.* Pacific Palisades, CA: Personal Strengths Assessment Service, 1973.

Powell, J. *The secret of staying in love.* Niles, IL: Argus, 1974.

Ringer, R. *Winning through intimidation.* New York: Fawcett Books, 1979.

Sherwood, J.J., & Glidewell, J.C. Planned renegotiation: A norm-setting OD intervention. In W.W. Burke (Ed.), *New technologies in organization development: 1.* San Diego, CA: University Associates, 1972.

Simons, G.F. *Keeping your personal journal.* New York: Paulist Press, 1978.

Simonton, C., Simonton, S.M., & Creighton, J. *Getting well again.* Los Angeles: J.P. Tarcher, 1978.

Smith, A. *Powers of mind.* New York: Ballantine, 1975.

Smith, M. *A practical guide to value clarification.* San Diego, CA: University Associates, 1977.

Thomas, K.W., & Kilmann, R.H. *Thomas-Kilmann Conflict Mode Instrument.* Sterling Forest, Tuxedo, NY: Xicom, 1974.

Tiger, L. Optimism: The biological roots of hope. *Psychology Today,* January 1979, pp. 18-33.

Van Nuys, D. Dealing with anger: Detachment or denial. *Human Behavior,* April 1975.

Walker, E.C. *Learn to relax.* Englewood Cliffs, NJ: Prentice-Hall, 1975.

Weller, S. Joseph Heller and Judith Viorst, humor can save your life. *Self,* August 1979, pp. 46-51.

Werthman, M. *Self-psyching: Thirty-five proven techniques for overcoming common psychological problems.* Los Angeles: J.P. Tarcher, 1978.